Wootton Courtenay

Dorothy Ball

Published in Great Britain in 2007

ISBN 978-0-9557385-0-0

Published by Peter Ball
25 Sunningdale Avenue
Ayr
KA7 4RQ
UK

Printed in Great Britain by Walker & Connell Ltd
Hastings Square
Darvel
Ayrshire
KA17 0DS

Contents

Plan of the Wootton Courtenay Estate, for sale in 1920

Foreword

Dorothy Ball was born Dorothy Mary Powell in 1917 in New Eltham, South London. Having met and married John Ball of Wootton Courtenay just after World War II, she gave up her teaching profession and became a resident of Wootton Courtenay, where she lived for her whole married life of nearly 60 years. She became very much part of the community in her many and varied roles, which included farmer's wife, Parish Council chairman and Women's Institute President.

She loved, and was fascinated by, the village, its history and its inhabitants. It is many years since she decided that she should search through the archives and through the memories of her friends and acquaintances in order to produce an account of the village and its history. Her task was almost complete when she died in 2005. We, her children - Peter, Martin and Mary - were determined that the result of her efforts should become available to anyone who was interested.

The book has been compiled from a variety of sources. Information from published work is cited in the text or in footnotes, and it will be obvious that a significant amount of information was gleaned from diligent searches of church, parish and other records.

Mum obtained a great deal of information from people who lived, or had lived, in the village. Many Wootton people, most of whom are no longer with us, told tales or passed on memories which Mum felt should be recorded.

Among them was Gwen Burnell, one of the area's great characters and a very long standing friend of the Ball family. She told Mum many good tales in her own inimitable style, often over a glass of sherry or at a family whist drive.

Bessie Dyke was a relative of our father, John. She was born and raised in Wootton Courtenay, but was living in Bristol when she got wind of the project and wrote to Mum, providing a great source of first hand memories from up to a century ago.

This is Mum's book, and I have tried, as far as possible, to retain the text as she wrote it. This means that some of the information is already out of date. Where I thought it essential, I have made minor amendments or added footnotes. I have also added a few sections on topics which we think Mum would have liked to include. In particular, with Brian Reed's help, I have added to Dorothy's information on the war years and created a chapter on that topic. The names of other contributors are shown in the text.

We have deliberately made no individual acknowledgement. Very many people have helped in a variety of ways to ensure that this book would be published, and we are deeply grateful to them. The problem we have is knowing who to thank. We therefore thank no-one in particular, but all of you heartily, hoping that everyone agrees that this is better than thanking some and leaving out others.

Almost all of the old photographs were in Mum's collection. We know who took some of them, but can only guess at the source of many of the others. Mum had lent some of them to other people, so that a few may have appeared elsewhere.

We hope that the book will bring back happy memories to those of you who knew Wootton Courtenay and be a source of interest to those who are new to, or visiting, this very special village. If enough of you buy it, any profits will be given to Wootton Courtenay Church.

Peter Ball

September 2007

One of Bessie Dyke's letters

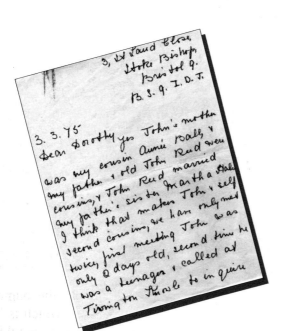

Wootton Courtenay

Wootton Courtenay is a village on the northern fringe of Exmoor and within the Exmoor National Park. It is five miles from Minehead, which was once a thriving port, commercial centre and Parliamentary borough and is now a tourist centre.

Wootton has remained a small rural community, dependent on agriculture until after the Second World War when it gradually changed to an almost entirely residential area sought after by retiring towns people.

Above: the village centre seen from across the valley

Below: Wootton Courtenay seen from the Brendon Hills with Grabbist to the right and the Vale of Porlock in the distance.

Yet in the early 21st century it could still be described as it was by James Savage in 1830: "The village of Wootton Courtenay is pleasantly situated on the very edge of the plain at the foot of the Grabist, facing Exmoor in the South; it forms a neat but irregular street, with its pretty neat Church and well kept Churchyard."*

In the Domesday book, the name of the village was 'Otone', which is how the present day 'Wootton' would be pronounced in the West Somerset Dialect.

One of the village's fields, known locally as 'Ood Ed', is actually 'Wood Head'). 'Courtenay' was added later, after the estate passed to the de Courtenay family in 1274.

* History of the Hundred of Carhampton, in the County of Somerset. By James Savage 662pp (1830)

Chapter One

Before the Norman Conquest

Evidence of neolithic man has been found. Flints of hunter's weapons were discovered by Laurie Bosley on land at Elsworthy, a farm in the parish on the fringe of Exmoor and flint tools used by farmers were dug up on lower land closer to the village by Peter Ball, who had them identified at Taunton Museum.

hillside today there is a thriving vineyard, run by Derek Pritchard, who says it is a very sheltered site - one of the few in England never to have suffered frost damage. It is also one of the steepest vineyards in England and has more than 1250 vines used to produce wine at the adjoining winery.

Flint flakes and tools found in Wootton Courtenay, including an arrow head (top left) and a scraper for cleaning hides (bottom right)

The Celts certainly had camps near Selworthy and settled on ridgeways, keeping as far as possible to high ground above forest and bog.

There are a few remains of Roman villas on Exmoor, and Roman coins have been found near Dunster. Vineyards were evidently cultivated on the hillside at Owey, north of Wootton, during the Roman occupation. On a similar nearby

During Saxon times, Exmoor was one of the 67 Royal Forests of England, its barren wastes offering no inducement to settlers who lived on lower ground where there was water and conditions were safer. Royal forests were not merely areas of woodland, but legal areas (including villages and fields) in which the King had sole privilege. Deer, boars and certain other wild animals, as well as the trees, were reserved for the King and protected by forest law. It was forbidden to keep dogs or possess bows and arrows within a forest. There were fines for making a hedge or cutting firewood and punishments for deer poaching. From 1508 Exmoor forest was leased for a rent to a warden who in turn let the land for grazing. It was also hunted. Struggling settlements developed in time. These later made up the parishes of Oare, Culbone, Porlock, Luccombe, Stoke, Wootton, Cutcombe, Exford, Winsford and Dulverton.

Otone was part of the Hundred of Carhampton. A Hundred was a military and taxation area consisting of one hundred Hides - a Hide (originally the name for a community or family group), being a section of land (between 60 and 120 acres) sufficient to support a warrior plus his family and dependants. Groups consisting of ten Hides each were organized by Tything men, who were responsible for law and order.

The Hundreds were grouped into threes, each group being responsible for the supply of a ship and a crew of sixty for the royal fleet.

During the 9th century King Alfred preserved what was left of Wessex around the marshes of Athelney in the Somerset Levels and gathered England's strength to give battle against the Danes. After much research the following interesting theory as to the involvement of Wootton Courtenay in this struggle has been suggested by Mr J. K. Riddler, (a resident of Wootton Courtenay for many years who was much interested in local history):-

Two Place-names of interest are Burrow, formerly "burgh", and Kingsbury, the latter being the name of fields south of Wootton Knowle homestead and below the road. They both appear to derive from the Saxon "burgh", a fortified place.

Across the head of the Porlock Vale from Knowle lies East Lynch, and behind it on a small plateau are the Danes Fields, from which Danes Lane leads up to North Hill at a point opposite the head of Henner's (Hinguar's?) Combe. It may well be that the Danes Fields are the site of a Danish camp and that Kingsbury is the "King's Burgh", an outpost of a main camp at Higher Burrow.

We know that in 878 King Alfred's men defeated the Danes at "Cynwit", which some have claimed to be Combwhich and others Countisbury or even Kingsbury. Asser's account of this fight says the Saxon camp was without water, and the nature of the ground rendered it safe except towards the east – this description fits Kingsbury. The Danish raiders laid siege to the camp and were overwhelmed by a sortie on the part of the Saxon soldiers, in which the Danish leader was killed.

It is noteworthy that beyond the Danes fields towards Selworthy are "How's Close" and "Cockrells" (field names), "how" being the Saxon word for burial place and "cock" the Danish. If it may fairly be claimed that Kingsbury is more likely to be the site of "Cynwit" than either of the others, it would be pleasant to think that our greatest English king won an important fight in this parish."

Chapter Two

The Manor of 'Otone'

Before and during the reign of Edward the Confessor (1042-66), the manor of Wootton was held by Algar, when it was known as Otone. This could have been a local pronunciation of Wootton possibly meaning "town in a wood".

The Saxon concept of land was that in general it belonged to the community, but after the Norman Conquest in 1066 all "unappropriated" lands were nominally owned by the King and could be distributed by him to his followers as a reward for services with the consent and approval of the Witan or wisemen members of the King's council, or 'moot' - who seem generally to have been his kinsmen or nominees.

After the Norman Conquest when William I became King he gave the manor of Otone to one of his followers, a French knight, William de Falaise. This is recorded in the Doomsday Book. This was a survey ordered by King William in 1086 and complied by the Treasury clerks at Winchester, of lands in England, the area of soil cultivated, names of landowners and the rights of Lords, tenants, money, structure of courts, value of mills, fish ponds, cattle etc.

The Doomsday Book still refers to 'Hides', but from this time the entity of Otone as a 'manor' emerged.

Ipfe.W.ten̄ *Ticheha*.Saulf 7 Teolf ten:b̄ T.R.E..p.ii.maner.
7 geldb̄ .p.viii.hid 7 dim̄.Tra.ē.ix.car̄.In dn̄io sf.iiii.car̄.7 iiii.
ferui.7 xii.uilli 7 v.bord cū.vi.car̄.Ibi.xxx.ac̄ pti.7 lx.ac̄
pafturæ.7 cx.ac̄ filuæ.Valb̄.c.fol qdo recep̄.Modo.vi.lib.

.XXIII.   **TERRA WILLI DE FALEISE.**
Willī de Faleise ten̄ *Stoche*.Brixi teneb̄ T.R.E.7 geldb̄
.p.iiii.hid 7 7 dim̄.Tra.ē.xiiii.car̄.In dn̄io sf.iiii.car̄.7 v.ferui.
7 xxxviii.uilli 7 iii.bord 7 iii.colib̄ti cū.x.car̄.Ibi molin̄ redd̄
xvi.den.7 cl.ac̄ pti.7 xix.ac̄ pafturæ.7 c.ac̄ filuæ.
Qdo recep̄.ualb̄.xxv.lib.Modo.xx.lib.
Huic m̄ addita.ē dimid hida.quā teneb̄ T.R.E. un̄ tain̄ in
paragio 7 poterat ire quo uoleb̄.Tra.ē.i.car̄.q̄ ibi.ē cū.i.bord
7 ii.feruis.Val sēp.x.folid.

96 d
Ipfe.W.ten̄ *Otone*.Algar teneb̄ T.R.E.7 geldb̄ .p.iii.hid.Tra.ē
x.car̄.In dn̄io sf.iii.car̄.7 vi.ferui.7 x.uilli 7 viii.bord cū.iiii.car̄.
Ibi molin̄ redd̄.x.den.7 iiii.ac̄ pti.Paftura.i.leū lḡ.7 dim̄ lat
7 tantd filuæ.Valuit 7 ual.c.folid.
Ipfe.W.ten̄ *Worspring*.cceffu regis.W.Serlo ded̄ ei cū fua
filia.Euroac teneb̄ T.R.E.7 geldb̄ .p.vi.hid.7 una v̄ tra.Tra.ē
xii.car̄.In dn̄io   Ibi.xiii.uilli 7 vi.bord hn̄t
vi.car̄.Ibi.x.ac̄ pafturæ 7 x.ac̄ filuæ minutæ.Sēp ual.c.fol.
Huic m̄.sf additæ.iii.hidæ q̄s teneb̄ T.R.E. Aluuard 7 Colo .p.ii.
maner.7 .p.iii.hid geldb̄.Tra.ē.viii.car̄.In dn̄io sf.iii.car̄.
7 iiii.ferui.7 vii.uilli 7 iiii.bord cū.iii.car̄.7 viii.ac̄ pafturæ.
Sēp ual.iiii.lib.

EXTRACT FROM

THE DOMESDAY BOOK

1086

96 c, d

« William holds TICKENHAM himself. Saewulf and Theodulf held it   E
before 1066 as two manors; they paid tax for 8½ hides.
Land for 9 ploughs. In lordship 3 ploughs; 4 slaves;
5 hides, less 1 furlong.   438
    12 villagers and 5 smallholders with 6 ploughs & 3½ hides & 1 furlong.   b 1
    Meadow, 30 acres; pasture, 60 acres; woodland, 110 acres.
    1 cob; 7 cattle; 7 pigs; 47 sheep.
Value when he acquired it, 100s; now £6.

[27]   LAND OF WILLIAM OF FALAISE

1 William of Falaise holds STOGURSEY from the King. Brictsi held   E
it before 1066; it paid tax for 4½ hides. Land for 14 ploughs.
In lordship 4 ploughs; 5 slaves; 2 hides.   369
    38 villagers, 3 smallholders and 3 freedmen with 10 ploughs   a 1
    & the rest of the land.
    A mill which pays 16d; meadow, 150 acres; pasture, 19 acres;
    woodland, 100 acres. 3 cobs; 29 cattle; 10 pigs; 250 sheep.
Value when he acquired it, £25; now £20.
    To this manor has been added ½ hide which a thane held   E
jointly before 1066; he could go where he would. Land for 1   E
plough, which is there, with
    1 smallholder and 2 slaves.
Value always 10s.

2 William holds WOOTTON (Courtenay) himself. Algar held it   96 d
before 1066; it paid tax for 3 hides. Land for 10 ploughs.
In lordship 3 ploughs; 6 slaves; 1 hide & 1 virgate.   369
    10 villagers and 8 smallholders with 3 ploughs & 2 hides.   a 2
    A mill which pays 10d; meadow, 4 acres; pasture 1 league
    long and ½ wide; woodland, as much. 1 cob; 13 cattle; 7 pigs;
    150 sheep; 18 goats.
The value was and is 100s.

3 William holds WOODSPRING himself, with King William's assent.   E
Serlo of Burcy gave it to him with his daughter. Everwacer held it
before 1066; it paid tax for 6 hides and 1 virgate [of] land.   369
Land for 12 ploughs. In lordship 4 hides & 3 virgates.   b 1
    13 villagers and 6 smallholders have 6 ploughs & 1½ hides.
    Pasture, 10 acres; underwood, 10 acres. 16 cattle; 92 sheep.
Value always 100s.
    To this manor have been added 3 hides which Alfward and Cola   E
held before 1066 as two manors; they paid tax for 3 hides.
Land for 8 ploughs. In lordship 3 ploughs; 4 slaves; 2½ hides.
    7 villagers and 4 smallholders with 3 ploughs & ½ hide.
    Pasture, 8 acres. 2 pigs.
Value always £4.

Copy of an extract from the Domesday Book of 1086, showing William de Falaise as owner of the manor of Otone

A manor is an English territorial unit, originally of feudal lordship, now consisting of the lords' demesns and of lands from whose holders he may extract certain fees etc. For many years the ownership of Wootton Manor passed by inheritance to the heirs of William de Falaise, until about the year 1240 when John Nevile gave Wootton land to his friend Sir Philip Basset. Sir Philip, before he died in 1274, bequeathed it to his granddaughter, Eleanor Despenser, on her marriage to Sir Hugh de Courtenay. From this time, Wootton has been called Wootton Courtenay (sometimes spelt Courtney). Hugh and Eleanor's son Hugh became the Earl of Devon whose heirs now live at Powderham Castle in Devon.

In Savage's book, "Hundreds of Carhampton" 1830, there are many pages relating to one squire, Henry Bilson Legge and from "The Diary of a Country Parson (James Woodforde)" by John Beresford (1924) we learn that:-

"Henry Bilson Legge was born in 1708, the forth son of the first Earl of Dartmouth. He owed his start in political life to Sir Robert Walpole to whom he was private secretary. In 1754 he became Chancellor of the Exchequer. In 1760 George III succeeded his grandfather and set about taking the lead in government, brooking no opposition, and in 1761 he dismissed Henry Bilson Legge because he refused to pay a large sum to the Landsgrave of Hesse. He shared in a measure of William Pitt's popularity whose colleague he was. If not an eminent statesman he was no fool."

There is no record, as far as we know, of Henry ever visiting Wootton. In fact from the time of the Conquest until the Estate was sold in 1921 there have always been absentee landlords so there has never been a manor house.

In 1779 Henry Bilson Legge married Mary, daughter of Viscount Curgon. She was created Baroness Stawell. When their son, Henry, Lord Stawell died in 1820, Wootton Courtenay land was left to his daughter, Mary, wife of John Dutton, only son of 1st Baron Sherborne and this family owned the manor until 1921 when the decision to sell the estate was probably due to a succession of deaths and the death duties involved.

In 1892 the Rev. the Hon. Frederick G. Dutton M.A. vicar of Bibury, Gloucester inherited the manor from his uncle Ralph. In 1901 he was made an Honary Canon of Gloucester Cathedral. He is remembered as a good landlord who visited the estate and was willing to spend money on improvements.

He built a house in Duck Street, Lower Town, named Brookside (now Riverside Farm) and let it to Mr and Mrs John Reed on condition that he stayed there when he visited the estate, often bringing his horses with him.

Mrs Reed cared for all his needs and used to tell how "Everything had to be done properly for Canon Dutton," including, one assumes, his meals, as he gave Mrs Reed a cookery book which was kept among the family treasures by her grandson, John Ball.

Stoneware used by Canon Dutton while he was staying at Brookside (now Riverside) Farm.

At this time the annual rents on the estate were paid to the estate agents, Messrs Hawkes and Andrew of Williton. An annual dinner was held at the cottage on Church Steps when the agent met the tenants where they partook of roast beef which in 1895 cost £1.5s. 6d. The beer cost 10s. 6d. and £1.17s. 0d. was paid to the cook. In 1978 Mrs Evelyn Parsons whose parents had lived in the cottage remembered her mother making the puddings and still possessed the recipe, a rich fruit pudding.

Having paid their rents and enjoyed a good meal the farmers and other tenants sat drinking beer and smoking the clay pipes they had been given.

Rent Dinner Pudding

2lbs moist sugar
2lbs finely chopped suet
2lbs sultanas
2lbs currants
1lb mixed peel
1lb flour
1lb breadcrumbs
1lb finely chopped almonds
2 apples chopped
8 or 12 eggs
4 lemons, grated rind and juice
4 nutmegs and spice
4 wineglasses of Brandy
(more if required)

Estate tenants enjoying their clay pipes

Rent dinner 1910
Back row: two gentlemen from Williton, Mr Yeandle (Mill Farm), Mr George Eames (Ford),
Mr Tomkins (Fairgarden), Mr Dascombe (Huntscott)
Seated: Mr Harry Reed, Mr Hosegood, Mr John Reed, Mr George Reed

For a complete history of Wootton Manor I recommend Geoffrey Stoat's book, "Lord of the Manor – an investigation into the ownership of the Manor of Wootton Courtenay 1066-1920." In his very thorough research, Geoffrey Stoat discovered the many interesting characters who have been associated with Wootton Courtenay's history- kings and queens, chancellors and judges, archbishops and ministers of the Crown – even a possible Pretender to the throne.

The sale of the Wootton Courtenay Estate in 1920

In 1919 Canon Dutton's brother died and he became the 5th Baron Sherborne, but in January 1920 he too died and the estate passed to his nephew James Huntly Dutton who immediately sold it to a firm of speculators who then put up for auction: "an Estate of 2,382 acres, the agricultural lands in the valley comprising some of the best in the country, the district being famed for its barley growing while the higher land provides very useful grazing."

SOMERSET

The Wootton Courtney Estate OF 2,382 ACRES

To be Sold by Auction,
On WEDNESDAY, APRIL 14th, 1921.
At 2 o'clock.
IN 53 LOTS.

Auctioneers
Messrs. NORBURY-SMITH & Co.
5, George Street,
Hanover Square, London, W. 1.

Solicitors:
Messrs. JOYCE, RISDON & HOSEGOOD,
Williton and Minehead,
Somerset.

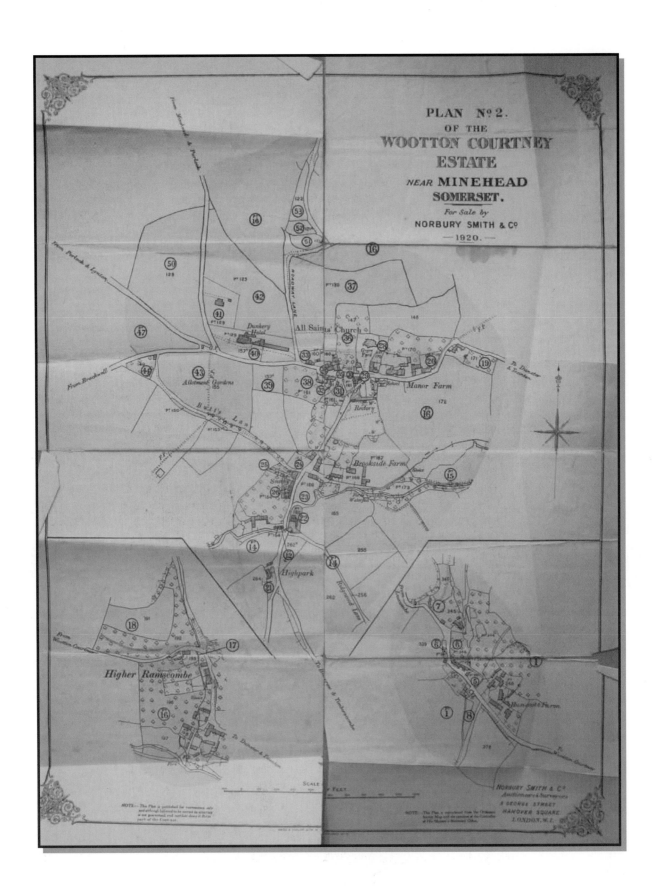

General View of Wootton Courtney.

Lot 1—Hunscott Farm.

Lot 2—Wootton Knowle Farm.

Lot 6.   Lot 5.
Cottages at Hunscott.

Lot 11—Stile Cottage.

Lot 12—Burrow Farm.

Lot 13—Ford Farm.

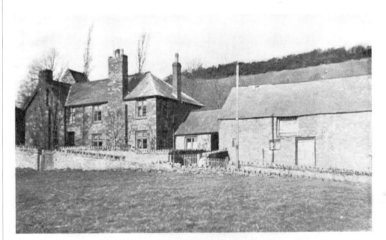

Lot 16—Manor Farm.

Lot 19—The Bakery.

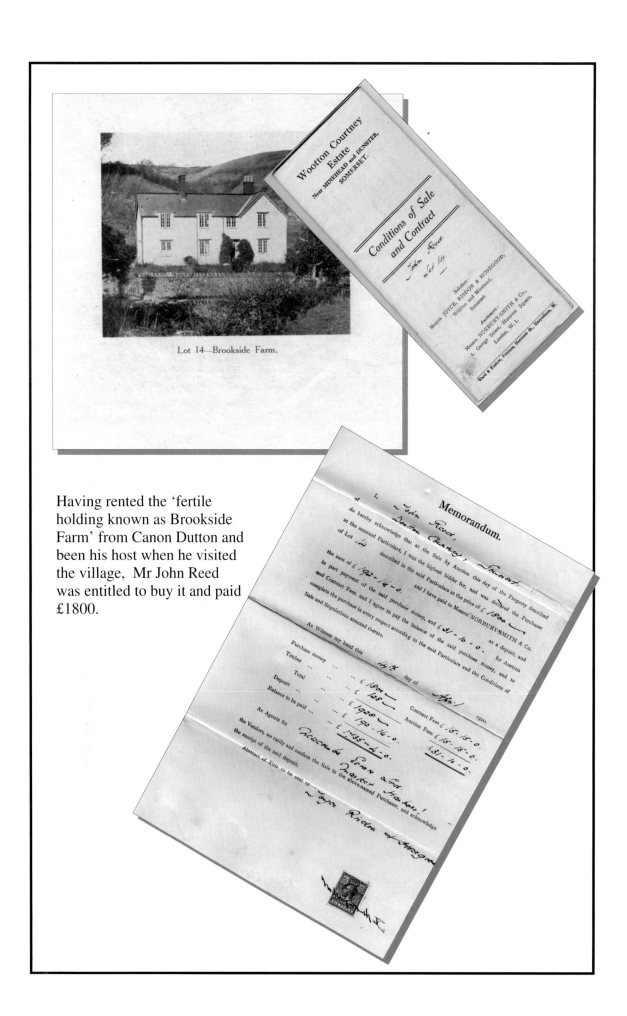

Lot 14—Brookside Farm.

Having rented the 'fertile holding known as Brookside Farm' from Canon Dutton and been his host when he visited the village, Mr John Reed was entitled to buy it and paid £1800.

John Reed also bought Highpark cottages and they became the workmens' tied cottages for the new Brookside Farm. The two cottages were turned back into one late in the 20th century and became John and Dorothy Ball's retirement home.

Lot 21

(Coloured BLUE on Plan No. 2.)

PARISH OF WOOTTON COURTNEY

A Pair of Well-placed Semi-detached

Cottages with Gardens

known as

J Reed.

"HIGH PARK COTTAGES"

160

having an area of about

38 Poles

(Numbered 264 on Plan).

Situate at the Southern end of the Village, on the Western side of the Wootton Courtney-Burrow Road.

They are stone built, with thatched roofs.

No. 1 contains: Two Bed Rooms, Living Room, with range, Scullery, Pantry.

Outside: Garden, stone and slate Outhouse, stone and tiled Pigstye, Closet.

Let together with other lands on lease for a term of 21 years, expiring Michaelmas, 1938, to Mr. John Reed, at an Apportioned Rental of £3 per annum.

No. 2 contains: Two Bed Rooms, Living Room, with range, Pantry.

Outside: Garden, stone built and slated Outhouse, stone built and tiled Pigstye and Closet.

This Cottage is in hand and possession will be given on completion of the purchase.

Water is obtained from the Rural District Council's supply at a tap outside each front door.

Commuted Tithe Rent Charge 8d.

Land Tax as assessed.

29

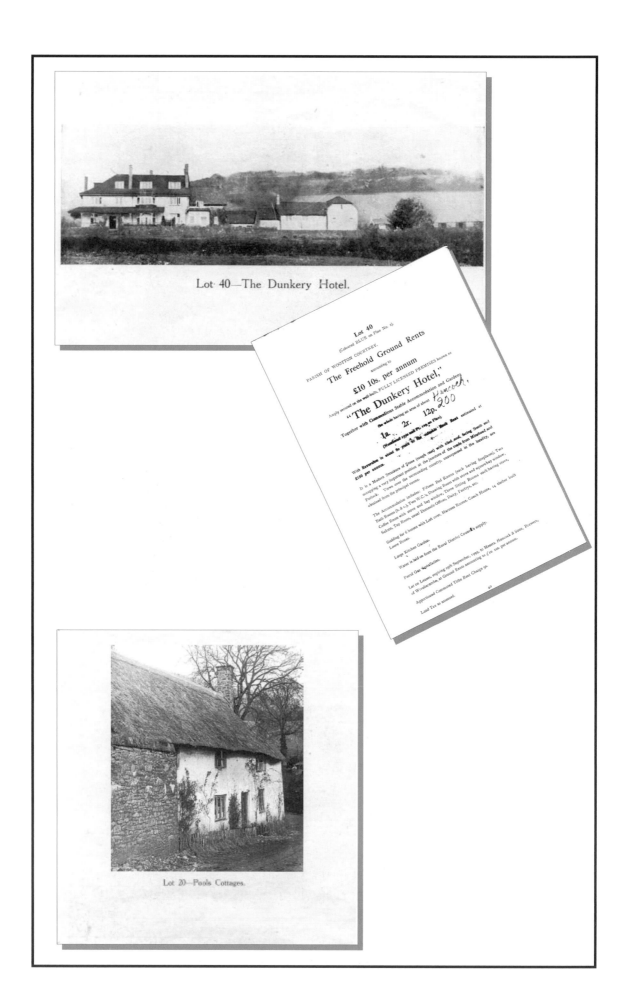

Lot 40—The Dunkery Hotel.

Lot 40
(Coloured BLUE on Plan No. 9).

PARISH OF WOOTTON COURTNEY.

The Freehold Ground Rents
amounting to

£10 10s. per annum

Amply secured on the well-built, FULLY LICENSED PREMISES known as

"The Dunkery Hotel,"

Together with Commodious Stable Accommodation and Garden,

the whole having an area of about *Hancock* 200

1a.   2r.   12p. (on Plan).

(Numbered type and Pt. 104 on Plan)

With Reversion in about 80 years to the valuable Hotel Rent estimated at
£180 per annum.

It is a Modern Structure of Stone (rough cast) with tiled roof, facing South and
occupying a very important position at the junction of the roads from Minehead and
Porlock. Views over the surrounding country, unsurpassed in the locality, are
obtained from the principal rooms.

The Accommodation includes; Fifteen Bed Rooms (each having fireplaces), Two
Bath Rooms (h. & c.), Two W.C.'s, Drawing Room with stove and square bay window,
Coffee Room with stove and bay window, Three Sitting Rooms each having stove,
Saloon, Tap Room, usual Domestic Offices, Dairy, Pantrys, etc.

Stabling for 6 horses with Loft over, Harness Room, Coach House, 14 timber built
Loose Boxes.

Large Kitchen Garden.

Water is laid on from the Rural District Council's supply.

Petrol Gas Installation.

Let on Lease, expiring 29th September, 1999, to Messrs. Hancock & Sons, Brewers,
of Wiveliscombe, at Ground Rents amounting to £10 10s. per annum.

Apportioned Commuted Tithe Rent Charge 9s.

Land Tax as assessed.

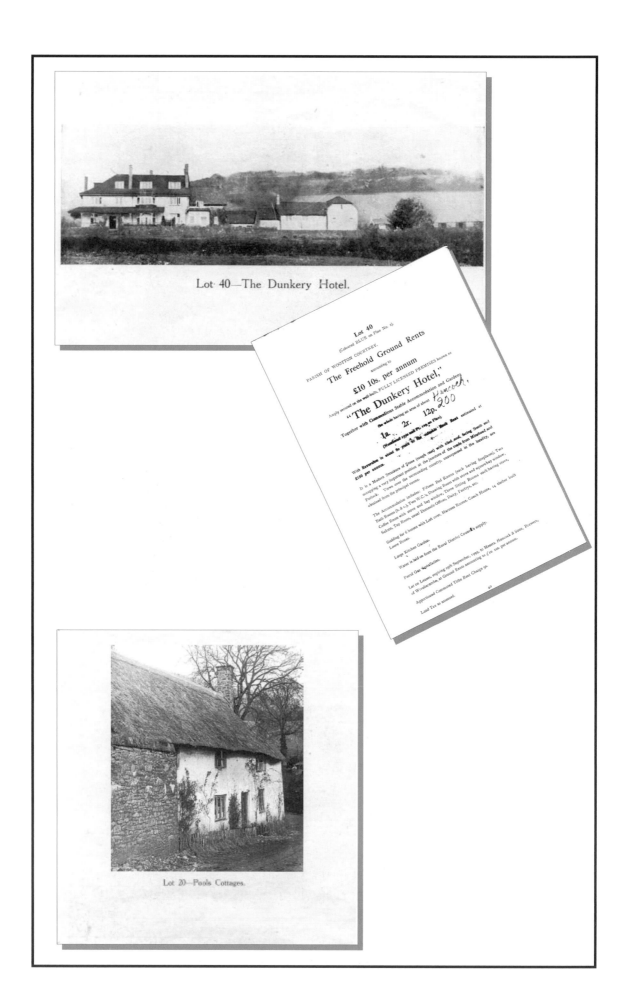

Lot 20—Pools Cottages.

Lot 23—Pair of Cottages.

Lot 26.   Lot 25.

Lot 28—Manor Cottage.

Chapter Three

Parish Records

On December 4th 1894 the first Parish meeting of Wootton Courtenay under the Local Government Act of 1894 was held in the School Room. Fourteen parochial electors were present and Rev. Stanley was elected chairman. Extracts from the minutes of meetings show aspects of village life over the last 100 years.

1897: Queen Victoria's Diamond Jubilee was celebrated. More of this in the chapter on social life.

1903: The proposed scheme of a water supply for the village was discussed and the meeting expressed the opinion that every effort should be made to bring the matter on as quickly as possible.

1909: The water supply should be extended to Fairgarden and Stile. Cannon Dutton (Lord of the Manor) guaranteed a payment of 5% of the cost for seven years, upon a reasonable outlay for the purposes. Then the water rate should be considered and a charge made of not less than 5% until the original outlay is paid off.

1923: There was a discussion about the dangerous corner at Ramscombe.

1924: Rubbish Disposal – it was decided that an application be made to the Rural District Council with a view to some definite arrangement being made for the disposal of rubbish instead of it being littered about the village.

1926: An application was made to the County Education Committee to supply such Library books on loan as in other places.

1927: A meeting was called to discuss the outlet of the main sewer which had been unsatisfactory for 22 years, but as the Sanitary Inspector had not attended as agreed, the meeting was postponed until he could attend.*

1928: A letter was sent to the Postmaster General asking that a motor cycle be supplied to the postman (Ivor Loveridge from Timberscombe) delivering letters and parcels to Wootton Courtenay in order that the mail should be delivered earlier.

1929: A letter was sent in reply to one from the National Council of Social Services that "While the people of Wootton Courtenay sympathised with the inhabitants of the distressed areas in the mining districts they can offer no house accommodation or employment at present." (In fact, two or three young men were given employment as "house-boys" in the village. Two were employed at Annicombe. One, Raymond Boycott, married a local girl and settled in the village, where his sons grew up).

Following a proposed scheme for the collection of refuse, permission was given by Mrs Hughes, owner of the site of one of the old iron pits (Higher Brockwell) to be used as a dump for unburnable rubbish.

Messrs J. Reed and Son offered to lend a horse and cart for collection of tins and bottles lying about the lanes. A "Jug and Bottle" committee was formed and people taking advantage of the monthly collection should pay a rate of 1d in the £ on the rateable value of premises.

*The sewer continued to empty into the River Hannay until at least the 1950's. We didn't worry! John Ball used to say "Running water purifies"

1930: The "Jug and Bottle" service was reviewed and it was agreed that it has proved a great success. Also on the agenda the need for more council houses was raised and there were openings for a carpenter and a shoemaker.

A twice-weekly bus service is in operation and a daily service promised for the near future. It was noted that several new houses have been built in the parish and others are contemplated, as the village is becoming an attractive residential resort.

1931: After several years of negotiations, a site has finally been agreed for the proposed Village Hall, as Mr John Reed has agreed to sell ¼ acre of land behind the Council Houses (in Stoney Close).

(Previously, a hut between Wreford and Fernlea in Higher Town, known as the Reading Room, had been used as a meeting place, mainly by young people, for social gatherings, games and cards. When the hall was erected, the old hut was attached to the new building and became the kitchen).

There was discussion on the possibility of obtaining a public electric lighting supply to the village. Later the meeting viewed with dismay the proposal to carry electric wires across the very fine scenery in front of the village and protests against the supply were made unless the wires were put underground.

1932: The meeting desired to place on record the profound disgust of the parish at Williton District Council's persistent mismanagement of the Wootton Courtenay water supply from the time when they built an unnecessary reservoir (on Exmoor above Ford Farm) and rendered it useless by piping the spring beneath it. (Previously the supply had depended on a few stones placed in an unprotected bog).

1937: An application had been made for a 10 mph speed limit through the village, but 30 mph signs had been put up by Somerset County Council of which members disapproved on the grounds that "motorists would drive too fast if they were allowed to travel as fast as that".

1938: A local ARP meeting was called and wardens and fire fighters enrolled. A first aid class was given by Dr Anderson (he lived at Allen's Meadow).

1939: There was concern at the dangerous way in which cars were parked in the centre of Higher Town near Church Steps and Somerset County Council were urged to paint white lines on the road.

1940: Weather report:- The stream in Lower Town was frozen over, so that several residents walked across it. The month was the coldest in memory of most people, 30 degrees of frost being registered in Higher Town.

These conditions, with heavy snowfalls and varying degrees of cold, lasted without a break from 9th January to 18th February.

1941: A fund was started to provide Christmas presents for the men of Wootton Courtenay who were serving in the forces.

On November 22nd the first Parish Council was elected with seven members. Mr John Ball was elected as Chairman. The West Somerset Free Press reported "Pursuant to the order made by the Somerset County Council some months ago, the people of this parish last Friday evening, elected the first parish council of Wootton Courtenay.

This was done by show of hands at a parish assembly, held in the village hall, and the momentous happening was all over in about three quarters of an hour.

Indeed, the procedure of electing a parish council for the first time can hardly have been carried out anywhere else in so smooth and efficient a manner as it was here - undoubtedly due to the preliminary care and attention of Mr C.T.F. Gibbs, chairman of the meeting and Mr Heasman, Chairman of the parish meeting. 70 out of Wootton Courtenay's electors were present.

The following were elected: N.J.H. Ball – farmer (59) Herbert Carter – master baker (50) Dudley Parsons – bus driver (49). Arthur Heasman – retired schoolmaster (44), Walter Conibere, Mason (42), William Middleton – road foreman (39), Albert Carter – gardener (38).

Chapter Four

The War Years

The war memorial in Wootton Courtenay Church, which records the names of those who served, were wounded and who died in the Great War.

Apparently only one villager was killed in the Second World War, although several were wounded.

Wootton Courtenay was well away from the thick of the World Wars, but a surprisingly high proportion of the village's young men played an active part, as the Church war memorial shows.

One example of service in the Second World War is found in the diary of John (Jack Junior) Reed of Higher Ranscombe Farm, who recorded his war Army Service as follows:

England	Sept 39 - Jan 42
Egypt	March 42 – May 42
Cyprus	May 42 – Jan 43
Libya	Jan 43 – March 43
Tunisia	March 43 – May 43
Egypt	May 43 – Aug 43
Palestine	Aug 43 – Oct 43
Syria	Oct 43 – Nov 43
Egypt	Nov 43 – Dec 43
Italy	Dec 43 – Nov 44
Greece	Nov 44 – Jan 46

His diary records the extensive training he received in England in 1941, whilst waiting for embarkation abroad.

Mention is made of some of this training at Grassington, Mapplewell and Wycombe.

Jack Reed Junior of Higher Ranscombe Farm in uniform during World war II

His involvement in the Eighth Army campaigns in North Africa and Italy, including the 'Battle for Monte Casino' must have been so different from his rural farming upbringing in West Somerset, yet as with many servicemen he didn't talk a lot about the war. His six year service took him to a very different world.

During his training year in 1941, his diary reports that on June 14th he 'went to hospital with measles' and stayed in hospital until 27th June.'

The only injury he sustained during the war years was in August, 1945. A doctor's note dated Oct 1945 confirms that a 'great swelling but no loss of consciousness' occurred and a 'depression of the frontal bone immediately above the nose' resulted. A surgical specialist was consulted for a second opinion. The cause…. misjudging the speed of a cricket ball when keeping 'wicket' to an army 'fast bowler' !

When he was 'demobbed' he returned to the family farm, married and continued to play a part in village life as cricket club chairman, church warden and local councillor.

These were the only times he ever left England in his 84 years.

Two brothers from the village - Ron and Charlie Baker - were sent to the front and were both blown up by a shell. By an amazing coincidence, they woke up in adjacent beds in a London hospital ward. The incident even made the national press, being reported in the Daily Mirror .

Another example of the hardships of the war was never forgotten by George Ball. He and his fellows lost their Christmas dinner when their American allies let down their guard whilst supposedly keeping the Germans at bay!

Farming was a reserved occupation, so that some, such as John Ball of Brookside Farm (grandson of John Reed, the subject of Chapter 12) had war-time duties in addition to maintaining production on the farms. He was an air raid warden.

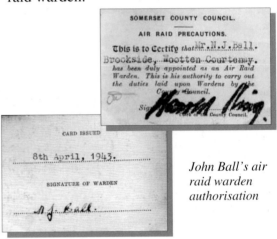

John Ball's air raid warden authorisation

Ron (left) and Charlie Baker, brothers from Wootton Courtenay- who ended their war service in adjacent hospital beds

Jack Reed Senior of Higher Ranscombe (John Reed's nephew), became the Civil Defence Warden. One of his jobs was to report any war related incidents. One interesting report is shown here.

Douglas Lang's father was involved in Home Guard horse patrol duties on North Hill and Grabbist. For camouflage purposes they needed a 'dark horse' Mr Docker's grey was too light in colour, and had to be painted brown. This was fine until heavy rain washed away half the paint, leaving the horse disguised as a zebra!

During World War II a number of children and their teachers were evacuated and billeted in the village, where they used the school. Some of the children, and some adults too for that matter, stayed for a very short time because they found the place too quiet!

A short record of High Explosive being dropped at Ranscombe, just outside Wootton Courtenay.

Gwen Burnell said:

"No, we didn't have evacuees. My aunty who farmed at Bagborough had a mother and two children staying with her and when the mother (who had a bakery shop or something in London) went back, they asked if Mother would take the children. They paid. It was private. And then the neighbour wanted to come, and Mother had three children for three years. They paid Mother privately. It was nothing to do with the government. She was allowed to have them. I still hear from the boys; two in Canada and one in Australia."

Above left:
    evacuee teachers with Mr C T F Gibbs (headmaster of Minehead Grammar School) and his wife (seated on right of photo).
Above right:
    evacuee children and their teachers at Wootton Courtenay School during the Second World War

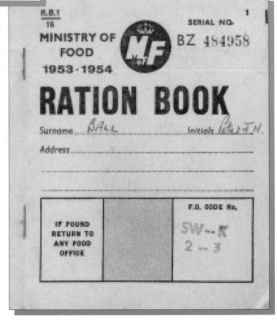

When the Second World War finished, the effects of it continued with rationing. Permission had to be obtained by John Reed to obtain potatoes.

Ration book for Peter Ball (age 5) for 1953-4

Chapter Five

Population

The first recorded account of the people of Otone was in the Doomesday Book when they lived in the hamlets which made up Otone (Wootton Courtenay): Ranscombe, Huntsgate (Huntscott), Wootton Ford (Ford), Brockwell and Burrow.

We learn that the population was:-

Villeins (Serfs)	10
Bordars (cottage owners)	8
Miller	1
Bondmen (slaves)	6

Wives and children were not listed. William de Falaise held Otone.

At this period there were still numbers of Saxon slaves, particularly dense in the West Country[*]. Villeins were feudal serfs or tenants who were subject to the lords or attached to the manor, and who could own no land.

It was not until the late 16th Century that parish records became available and there was a greater opportunity to study the populations of town and village communities. The first entry in the church register was in 1558.

In 1641/2 a record of Wootton Courtenay parish lists 93 men over 18 years. "88 in the same hand – 5 are signatures:"

John Morley – Rector

Robert Coffin; Robert Court
        (Churchwardens)
John Westcott; John Wheddon
        (Overseers)

During the commonwealth period from 1645 to 1660 parish records were neglected, possibly due to the plague. In 1645, the death rate in Minehead and district rose to about five times that of the normal rate. The churchwarden's account book in 1656 records a large number of burials, again probably as a result of plague.

In 1662 a tax was levied on houses based on the number of chimneys. It could be avoided by the blocking of chimneys. In Wootton Courtenay the records show that in 1662 there were 200 people living in houses large enough to pay tax on one chimney, but there is no evidence of the number too poor to pay. John Hole is recorded as having paid tax on four hearths.

In the 1660s, the recorded population of Wootton was smaller than it had been in 1641. This may have been partly due to the plague, but also because a number of homesteads were evading the hearth tax and so were not recorded.

In Dwelly's Hearth Tax Returns for 1664-5, 43 houses were recorded in Wootton Courtenay. These included:-

John Wheddon: 8, but paid one too many by mistake

John Westlake: 2- he hath let out one to a very poor tenant in distress and owner refuses to pay it

(James?) Valentine: 4- He hath stopt up one

John Oliver: 0- not worth 20s p. annie

John Hole: -4-

[*]Could this be why some still think that West Country folk are dense!?

In 1791, the number of houses in the village was about 54, with 250 inhabitants. Thirty houses formed a neat, though irregular, street near the church. The rest were distributed in the following hamlets:-

Wootton Ford: 3
Huntsgate (Huntscott)   8
Brockwell: 2
Burrow: 3

Hopcott and Periton were once part of the parish of Wootton Courtenay, but are now part of Minehead, whilst Bratton was passed to the Earl of Lovelace's family in 1733.

Population census returns help to give us a general picture of life in the 19th Century. The first census was taken in 1801, when the population was 345, with 81 families.

The following is the 1821 return for Wootton Courtenay:-

Houses inhabited	57
Families	81
Of whom employed in:	
Agriculture	64
Trade	14
Other	3
Persons	411
Males	215
Females	196

This shows an increase in twenty years of 66 persons and also indicates that farming was the main occupation.

In 1834 Mr Eames and his family farmed at Ford Farm*. The following is part of an old bill for work done for him by Geo. Burnell, carpenter.:-

Work for:-
   Mr Eames 1834
      To Geo Burnell - Carpenter

	£	S	d
For 1 day and half sawing		4	0
John 2 days making hurdles		2	8
Making a cart and finding part of timber		10	0
2 days myself and James to work in house		6	4
1 day James and John haymaking		1	8
John 3 days harvest		2	6
For family cart wheels		4	6
For making two milk jels			
Sawing finding part of timbers		5	6
For the cart saffs carriage		8	6
Making a cart 10/- Finding lades 1/6		11	6
For 9 vellows and 11 spokes for wheels	1	1	6
	6	9	0

*The 1881 census records the Eames family still farming at Ford. Old George and then his sons George and William and daughter Emma farmed there until 1940. George and his brother and sister, wishing to retire, sold the farm, which continued to be farmed, together with Brook-side Farm, by the Ball family. George and his brother and sister retired to 3 Bishops Cottages in Lower Town.

A more detailed picture of the parish can be gathered from the 1861 census return which appears to be the work of the 19 year old son of farmer Thomas Bowering of Middle Borough and the registrar who checked it was probably Dr Hole from West Harwood.

PARISH OF WOOTTON COURTENAY
Census 1861

Hunscott	9 households (2 farmers, 1 grocer, 1 dressmaker)
Ford	4 families
Elsworthy	2 families
Mill	2 families (including "Mrs Westcott, milleress")
Spangate	1 family

Inhabited houses	73
Males	205
Females	173
Total population	378

Agricultural labourers	58	
Carters	12	
Farmers	12	
Domestic service	12	
Dairymaids	4	
Shepherds	2	
Farmhouse manager & housekeeper	2	
Boot and shoe makers	2	
Sawyers	3	
Shopkeepers	5	
Dressmakers	2	
Farm servants	3	
Washerwomen	2	
Milleress	1	(head of household)
Miller	1	(son)
Cordwainer	2	
Schoolmistress	1	
Masons	3	
Tailors	3	(W &G Burnell &Hugh Roberts)
Carpenters	6	
Gardener	1	
Innkeeper	1	(David Knight of the Rose and Crown)

This record shows that the majority of the population (about 100) was still mainly engaged in farming and associated trades. It is interesting to see that the mill, recorded in Doomsday returns, was still working under the ownership of Mrs Westcott, the milleress.

In 1978, Mr Jan Ridler told me that his father remembered when the mill was working and that grist corn was obtained from Periton by the villagers, who took it to the mill to be ground into flour. At that time labourers were allowed to buy corn, not necessarily the best, but often the rakings from the field after the bulk of the crop had been taken away. These rakings had at times lain in the fields and become wet and practically useless.

The mill wheel was removed during the First World War, but the old mill still exists. The mill house became a farm and in the 1881 census return Robert Greenslade was listed as Farmer, Head of Household of Wootton Mill Farm. It remained a farm until Michael Gaitskell converted it to a pottery in 1974 and reconstructed a working water wheel where he continues to produce attractive stoneware sold locally and abroad.

Mill Farm after 1974. Rosemary Gaitskell relaxes

The new mill wheel

During the latter part of the 19th century, the population in England declined during a period of agricultural depression and we read of poverty among rural communities throughout the country. In Wootton Courtenay it was reported in 1872 that the average wages had been as low as eight shillings a week, with sometimes the addition of two pints of cider a day. Most labourers paid a shilling a week rent for a cottage, though one man with a wage of six shillings was given a cottage rent free*.

Some cottages had gardens, but most farmers gave their workmen a strip of ground in which to grow potatoes. This custom was still in practice until after the Second World War. In Wootton Courtenay, most labourers also rented an allotment or "garden" as it was called on which to grow extra root crops, from the landlord, Lord Sherborne. Some of these gardens can still be seen on the slopes of Wootton North Hill.

There are others north of Woodcock Lane, which was originally a packhorse and bridle path. A Wootton Courtenay tithe award in 1844 records "365 Lord Sherborne, Land worked over for iron stone 9 acres, 2 rods, 12 perches" The adjoining land was still in hill gardens.

Five of these gardens now form the Woodcock Lane nature reserve. They were cultivated for some years after 1920, when John Reed bought them at the auction of the estate after which they gradually reverted to moorland and scrub.

In 1936 John Reed sold them to Aubrey Cartwright, who hoped to build a house there. Access and water supply made this impossible, so he sold the land to Douglas Gibbs, son of the first headmaster of Minehead Grammar School, who lived in Brockwell Lane.

In 1990, Dr Gibbs offered it to the Exmoor Natural History Society as a nature reserve, which was managed for many years under the enthusiastic leadership of Malcolm Scott.

Woodcock Lane Nature Reserve in 2007

*The Romance of a Peasant Life in the West of England, 1872 by F.J. Heath

Until 1871 there had been a more or less continual increase in the size of the population of Wootton Courtenay, but the 1881 census shows a decline, which continued during the agricultural depression. In 1891, the inhabitants numbered 297 and in 1901 only 264 were listed. Bessie Dyke, in her letter remembered that "in 1900 a large part of the village was owned by Canon Dutton. Population around 200; children 40 to 50 mark. Rector, farmers, estate tradesmen, farmworkers comprised the population."

Children of Lowertown circa 1900

Front row :   *Louis Davis, Sally Kingdon, Freddy Pugsley, Jimmy Pugsley, Daisy Hole,*
                Violet Hole, Lily Davis, Ernie Davis.
Middle row: *George Davis and Bill Childs*
Back Row: *Mrs Ferris, Redvers Palmer, Pheobe Palmer, Leonard Roberts, Benny Bowditch,*
                Reg Bowditch, Mrs Vaulter, Manel Roberts, Mrs Bowditch,,
                Mrs Davis, Edward Childs, Emmie Childs and Mrs Childs.
Mr Bowditch is standing in Tom Court's doorway

Lowertown residents in the late 1890's

Background: Alf Court (with pickaxe), Mr Phelps, Sam Baker and Jim (Jumbo) Bailey.

*Foreground: Mrs Priscott, Bill Smith (the Smith's nephew), Harry Priscott (the smith), George Morgan,
Harry Roberts, Will Braunton, Mrs Dave Roberts (with Leonard), Mrs Morgan with 'Nettle',
Jim Morgan (carpenter) and George Williams.*

By 1971, the return gives the total population as 243, with 95 men, 118 women plus 12 boys and 18 girls under 18 years. The number of households had increased to 110 as a number of new houses had been built between the two world wars along Ranscombe Road, New Road and Brockwell Lane. The size of the population has not varied greatly for many years, but from being a community almost entirely dependant on agriculture until around the time of World War Two, it has become a much sought after residential area, mainly for retired people. However, at the beginning of the 21st Century there is a thriving village shop, with a post office and tea garden and several other family run enterprises including a vineyard, a pottery, beekeeping, painting and decorating, carpentry and furniture making. The population in 2001 was 280, in 144 households.

Chapter Six

The Poor

After the suppression of the monasteries the law had made parishes responsible for the impotent poor. Two overseers of the poor were appointed by the vestry, whose duty it was to levy a poor rate and supervise its distribution. In 1776, Wootton had a workhouse which could accommodate 16 people. This poor house consisted of five cottages where Jasmine Cottage now stands. Charity money given to the poor in that year was recorded as £61.15.11d.

In 1785 it was £95.17.0d, while in 1803 money for the poor raised by parish rates was £165.1.6d (3s.2d in the pound).

The following copies of documents which were stored in the church tell us of one problem dealt with by the churchwardens and overseers of the poor of Wootton in "1745, year of George 2nd" It was not until 1752 that England adopted the Gregorian calendar. Before that, the beginning of a new year was in March.

DISTARGE

To the churchwardens and other overseers of the poor of the parish of Selworthy and to the churchwardens, overseers of the parish of Wootton Courtenay to receive and obey.

Whereas complaints have been made by you, the churchwardens and overseers of the parish of Selworthy aforesaid that Joan Brook, single woman, has lately intruded herself into your said parish of Selworthy, there to inhabit as parishioner, contrary to the laws relating to the settlement of the poor and is likely to become chargeable to your said parish of Selworthy. We therefore upon due examination and inquiry made in the premises aforesaid (upon oath)... that you do forthwith convey her, the said Joan Brook from your parish of Selworthy to the parish of Wootton Courtenay ....and the churchwardens and overseers of the poor are required in his Majesty's name to provide for her.

7th day of February 1745, year of George 2nd

MAINTENANCE

To the churchwardens and other overseers of the poor of the parish of Selworthy and to the churchwardens, overseers of the parish of Wootton Courtenay to receive and obey.

Whereas Joan Brook of the parish of Wootton Courtenay was on or about the 11th day of March, delivered of a male bastard child within the parish, which child is now living and chargeable to the parish of Wootton Courtenay and likely to continue and we do adjudge John Brewer of Timberscombe, labourer, to be the father of the said child and for the relief of the said parish also for provision and maintenance of the said bastard child, we order the said John Brewer shall weekly and every week from the birth of the said child for as long as the same child shall be chargeable to the said parish
(then follow details of amounts payable)

March, 1745

Somerset:- To all constables, petty constables and tything men within the said county:-Whereas - Joan Brooks - single woman has this day made oath before me, one of his majesty's justices of the peace for the said county:-

that she was on or about the 17th day of March delivered of a male bastard child within the parish of Wootton Courtenay, which said child is still living and likely to become chargeable to the said parish of Wootton Courtenay and has on her oath charged John Brewer of Timberscombe in the county of Somerset that had begotten in her body the said male bastard child of which she was delivered aforesaid.

The churchwardens and overseers of the poor of this parish of Wootton Courtenay have this day applied to me for my warrant for the immediate apprehending the said John Brewer being the putative father of the said male bastard child

...........He is to be apprehended...... in order to give security to indemnify the said parish of Wootton Courtenay, the parishioners and inhabitants thereof.

1745, in the year of George 2rd.

Writing of poverty in 1872, FJ Heath said "The poor of Wootton Courtenay always had the support of the rector, Right Reverend James Chapman, and his curate, Rev. Charles Sainsbury, who provided active sympathy and help in any case of distress. In addition, the rector kept a small herd of cows and gave the milk to the poor. Extra money could always be earned at harvest time.

Meanwhile, George Joyce of Winsford, in his will of 1652, left property for the equal benefit of the poor of the parishes of Winsford, Cutcome and Wootton Courtenay after his wife's death. According to W. Dicker (1900)* Joyce died the following year and his wife died in 1683. "A decree, or decretal order, of the high court of chancery was obtained in 1691, in which it was ordered and directed that the said lands and premises should be conveyed to the churchwardens and overseers of the said parishes, and to their heirs for and on behalf of and said poor people, according to the Will and desire of the said George Joyce, deceased.

Fifteen trustees, or feoffees were chosen, five from each parish to manage the said charity, and they were required from time to time for ever thereafter in Easter week yearly to account with the churchwardens and overseers of the poor of the several parishes for the rents and profits by them received or made or the said lands and premises, i.e. The farm known as East Nurcott, in the parish of Winsford". (Joyce apparently owned this farm freehold. Ford and (North) Hawkwell in Cutcome parish, also mentioned in the will, were probably held on leases for lives). It appears that the trustees were never legally appointed until 1914, when the situation was formalised by the charity commission.

In 1750, 41 poor people in Wootton Courtenay received a total of £4.16.0 and in 1894, 37 received £20.19.0.

*DICKER, W, "Notes on the history of Winsford", Proceedings of the Somerset Achaeological and Natural History Society vol. 46 (1900) pp.188-195

In the Name of God. Amen. The seaven=
teenthe day of May in the year of o:r Lord God.
One thousand. sixe hundred. fifty and two.
I. George Joyce. of the pish of Winsford. in the
Countie of Somerset. yeoman. beinge sicke of
bodye. but of good and perfect memory. thanks
be unto the Almightie God. do constitute. and
ordayne this my last Will and Testament in
manner and forme as followeth. First I doe
bequeathe my soule into the hands of my
Lord and Saviour Jesus Christ. And my bodye
to the christian buryall. I give to the poore of the
parishes of Winsford. Calcombe. and Wotton
Courtny. equally betweene those three parishes
poore people all my land lyeing and beinge in
the pish of Winsford in a village called or knowne
by the Name of Horcott after the decease of my Wife
Elinor Joyce and to remain unto them forever.
And I give unto them my two tenements lyeing in
the pish Calcombe called by name of Hawchiwell
and Ford after the decease of my Wife if Robert
Severis doe over live her for the whole tearme
life. I give unto him my tenement at Luxborow
called ferley lately in the or occupacon of William

Butcher, and they shall have that after the fire
and twentith day of March next ensuinge
duringe the whole tearme that I have in it.
I give them all the houshold stuffe which is in
my house or the value thereof after the decease of
my Wife. Item. I give them all the money
which is owed unto me reserveinge inough to
my Executrix to make out three sets of silver
buttons. I doe intreat William Edbrooke of Winsford
Michael Hole of Wootton Courtny and John
Thorne of Calcombe. to make the best use and
benefitt they cann of their legacies given to the
poore of those three parishes. and for their pa___
I give unto them one set of silver buttons ap___
I give unto my God children. Ten shill___
my Will is that M:r Kinn my landl___
have my red cow. and foure po___
money at my death for Heriotts ___
my goods and chattels not given no___
ed my debts and legacies payd. my ___
charges defrayed I give & bequeathe unto ___
Wife Elinor Joyce to whome I doe make consta___
and ordayne whole and sole Executrix of this m___
last will and Testament whereunto are Witnesses

May 17:th 1652.

This is the
Last Will
and
Testament
of
George Joyce.

William Edbrooke. Christopher Hobbs after the
death of those three men here named my Will
is that the wardens and overseers of those three
parishes shall have the ordringe of those
legacies for those poore.
George Joyce

COPY OF THE LAST WILL AND TESTAMENT OF GEORGE WILLIAM JOYCE -

May 17th 1652

In the names of God Amen, the Seaventeenthe day of May in the year of our Lord God One thousand six hundred fifty and two, I, GEORGE JOYCE, of the parish of Winsford in the County of Somerset Yeoman, beinge sick of body but of good and perfect memory thanks be unto the Almightie God do constitute and ordaine this my last Will and Testament in manner and Form as followith. First I doe bequeathe my soul unto the hands of my Lord and Saviour Jesus Christ and my body to the Christian burail. I give to poor of the parishes of Winsford Calcombe and Wotton Courenty equally between those three parishes poor people all my land lyeing and beinge in the parish of Winsford in a village called or known by the name of Norcott after the decease of my wife Elinor Joyce and to remain unto them forever and I give unto them my two tenements lying in the parish Calcombe called by name of Hawckwill Calcombe Ford after the decease of my wife if Robert (? - Will torn) doe overlive her for the whole tearme of life I give unto him my tenement at Luxborough called Perley lately in the or oceupatfon of William Butcher they shall have that after the five and twentieth day of March next ensuinge duringe the whole tearme that I have in it. I give them all the household stuffe which is in my house or the Value thereof after the decease of my wife. Then I give all the money which is owed unto me reservinge enough to my Executrix to make out three sets of silver buttons I doe entreat William Edbrooke of Winsford Michael Hole of Wootton Carney and John Thorne of Calcombe to make the best use and benefit they canne of their legacies given to the poor of those three parishes and for their pains I give unto them one set of silver button apiece. I give unto my God Children ten shillings a piece .my Will is that Mr.Pinn my landlord shall have my red cow and four pounds in money at my death for. Herriotts. The rest of my goods and chattels not given nor bequeathed my debts and legacies payd my funeral charges defraued I give & bequeathe unto my wife Elinor Joyce whome I do make constitute and ordayne whole and sole Executrix of this my last Will and Testament whereunto are witnesses William Edbrooke Christopher Hobbs. After the death of those three men here named my will is that churchwardens and overfees of those three parishes shall have the orderinge of those legacies for those poor.

GEORGE JOYCE

The text of Joyce's will

Michael Hole, of Wootton Courtenay, was one of those charged in the Will to "make the best use and benefit they canne of their legacies given to the poor of those three parishes." It seems that his descendants remained involved in the administration of the bequest as the following letter to "I Hole Esqre and the Churchwardens and overseers of the parish of Wootton Courtney" indicates.

Copy of letter from George Orchard (right) and cover letter from Bristol Royal Infirmary (below and below right)

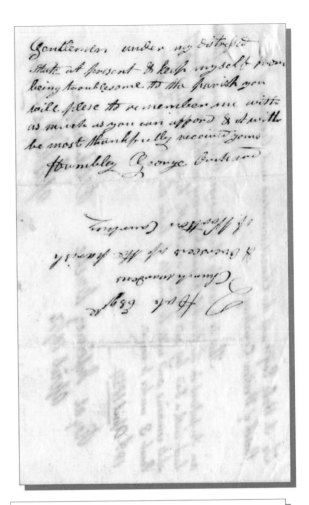

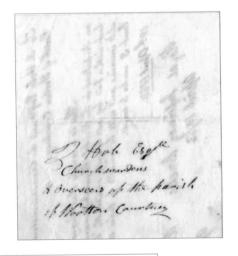

Gentlemen under my distressed state at present to keep myself from being troublesome to the parish you will plese to remember me with as much as you can afford & it will be most thankfully received. Yours humbly George Orchard

To "I Hole Esqre and the Churchwardens and overseers of the parish of Wootton Court-ney.

This is to certify that George Orchard was admitted an inpatient in the Bristol Royal Infirmary on the 5th February last with a bad leg and having accidentally broken his thigh he still remains and will be unable to leave the infirmary for at least three weeks to come   18th April 1854

William Hole of Alcombe was almost certainly a descendant of Michael Hole. The codicil to his will of 25th June 1860 contains the following extract:-

...all the rest... I give to my sister Lucy Hole* for her life...and (then) the said household goods and furniture, plate, wine and books shall be sold, ... The money to arise from the sale thereof I give as follows namely.....the remaining third be paid to such of the trustees of the Poor Land belonging (in part) to the Parish of Wootton Courtenay, as are elected for Wootton Courtenay in trust for the poor of Wootton Courtenay.......

The money is to be invested in the funds and the income is to be distributed about Christmas yearly to the indigent poor in blankets, bedding or warm clothing or in bread.

In 1871, Hole's bequest consisted of Government Bonds to the value of £956 - enough to buy 20 houses! The income of £27.4s.10d provided blankets etc. for 52 people. The capital never increased and the £24.11s.6d raised in 1965 provided 11 families with a pair of sheets each. By 2004, £22.48p was less than the cost of administration, so the bonds were transferred to the Village Hall fund and Hole's bequest was wound up.

Meanwhile, the rent obtained from East Nurcott Farm (Joyce's bequest) had become uneconomic and the trustees rationalised the situation, renting the farmhouse separately as a dwelling, and the land to a neighbouring farm This approximately doubled the income, raising sufficient funds to improve the house and provide a shed on the land, as well as providing more money for the bequest. There were 34 recipients in 1895 and 4 in 2007

* Lucy was born in Wootton Courtenay and there is a stained glass window in the north aisle of the church dedicated to "L.Hole"

AGRICULTURE

Until the last years of the 20th Century, agriculture has been the principal occupation of the inhabitants of Wootton Courtenay. In Britain, apparently, man first started to cultivate land from Neolithic times (about 2,500BC). At some stage he discovered that land became more fertile where there was ash after foliage had been burned and he was able to produce more food for himself and the animals he was now rearing. One of the ways in which archaeologists locate an ancient settlement is by noting the darkness of the soil Sometimes a place or field name which contains the word black refers to the ash stained soil near an old settlement. Flints were found in the vicinity of a field called Blackland on Ford Farm on the lower slopes of Exmoor.

In Laurence Meynell´s book, "Exmoor" we read that the Celts who had camps near Selworthy apparently grew barley, wheat and beans in fields ploughed by oxen. Until the late 20th century the fertile Porlock Vale area was known worldwide for its award winning barley.

From early times, where a Christian Church existed in a village, it was provided for by being allotted one virgate (30 acres) of land free of services. A normal holding had villanes (villagers) who supplied two oxen to help pull a common plough over strips of land scattered through common fields. Thus the early scheme of agriculture was truly co-operative. The allotment to the church of the produce of every tenth strip of land was the origin of the "Tithe" a right which was subsequently extended (justly or otherwise) to cover not only land, but animals and other produce.

In 1086 the Doomsday survey records "Oton" as having land for ten ploughs, four acres of meadows; pasture one league long and half a league wide; woodlands as much; one cob; thirteen cattle; seven pigs; one hundred and fifty sheep; eighteen goats (i.e. mixed farming as it remained for centuries). Probably Dunster was already the centre of a thriving wool industry.

From the Exeter Doomsday survey we learn "Warine FitzGerald holds Wootton which belongs to his barony of Stoke Courcy*. A few horses were kept, a large number of goats and the business of agriculture performed by oxen. The orchards produce mainly cider apples which are allowed to fall off the trees and placed in heaps to ferment."

Somerset cider has never been produced for sale in Wootton, but most farms had an orchard and owned a cider press where their apples and those gathered by neighbours were crushed into juice for cider making.

*Warine FitzGerald inherited the manor when he became the second husband of Alice de Curci, a descendant of William de Falaise

John Ball recalls that when he was a boy in the 1920's he and the other village lads used to take apples to Jack Reed's farm at Ranscombe to be crushed in the press. Until it was nine days old the boys were allowed to sample the juice. Mature cider was not for the likes of them!

Norman kings loved hunting and their ownership of "unappropriated" land, which was often waste land, became more and more accepted as being supreme, though inhabitants of bordering hamlets had, in the meantime, established rights of common and could turn out sheep and cattle and gather fuel. A "forest" – not necessarily an area of woodland – was a district in which deer and certain other wild animals were reserved to the king and protected by forest law. Wootton people had rights in the Forest of Exmoor.

In the reign of Edward III, it had become practice for wardens of the forest to hold inquisitions as to trespasses committed in the forest: "Hugh de Courtenay, Lord of Wootton, and their men and tenants enter the forest aforesaid with their cattle and in the same (graze?) the herbage of the Lord King, by what warrant is not known."

Towards the end of the sixteenth century, deer and certain other wild animals in the forest, though reserved to the king, were becoming exterminated due to the increase of people, but were still protected by forest law. In Elizabeth's reign, two cases in the records of the Court of Star Chamber, show that the Warden of Exmoor claimed deer in the forest. One case was against a servant of Mr George Lutrell of Dunster Castle for killing deer and taking calves to stock Dunster Park on several occasions at Oare, Luccombe and Wootton Courtenay. Mr Lutrell claimed a right to hunt deer throughout the Hundred of Carhampton.

In 1736, the original account books of the deputy forester afford some interesting particulars about the forest and its revenue at that time. Payment for pasturing sheep formed by far the greatest bulk of what the warden of the forest enjoyed. There is a list of sheep arranged under owner's names and marks, numbers of their sheep and sum payable, together with the portion of the forest where sheep were put. This is followed by another list of bullocks, in all 127 of which 112 belong to commoners at one shilling apiece and the remaining fifteen to strangers at two shillings. Wootton Courtenay was represented.

It is possible, although there is no proof, that at one time there was a toll gate at the now derelict Spangate Farmhouse on the eastern side of Dunkery Hill in Wootton Courtenay parish, recorded in an 1844 tithes survey as a farmhouse with 106 acres of land and shown on a 1903 map as an oval enclosure with earthwork, ruined building and spring. However, I wonder if this was a 'Telling House'. Sheep were put into the forest in March or May and stayed until driven away by their owners at shearing time. 'Tellers' were appointed to count the sheep as they left and toll collected. Unauthorised stock was charged double rates.

The final perambulation was made under which the provisions of the Enclosure Act settled once and for all the legal boundary of the old forest and the modern Parish of Exmoor in 1815*. Wootton Courtenay was named in the final Act of Enclosure but no allotments were made in respect of the old tenements, probably because the occupiers had not turned their sheep into

*The perambulation of the Royal Forest of Exmoor was re-enacted for a few years in the 1960's and again in recent years

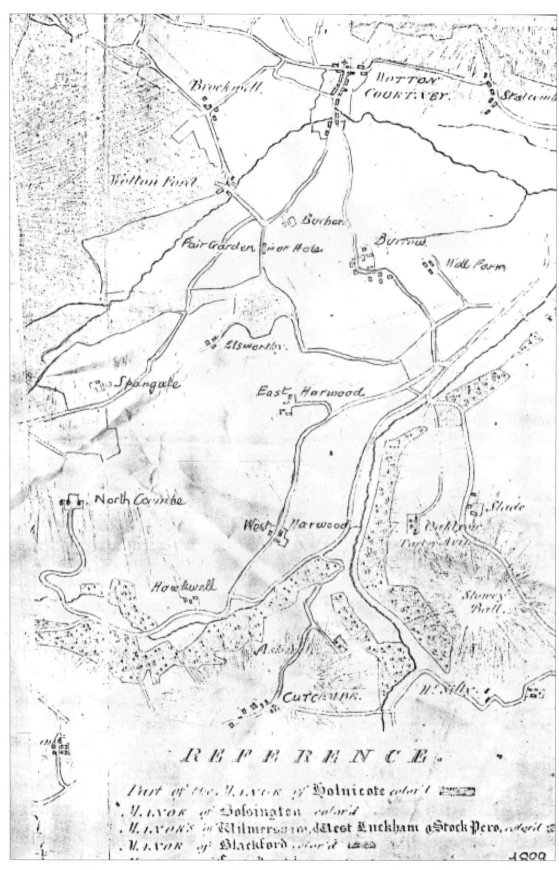

Copy of an 1889 map showing farms to the South of the Village following the
enclosure awards for Wootton Manor in 1872

the forest for many years, and were considered to have relinquished their rights. The date of the enclosure awards for Wootton Courtenay manor was 3rd October 1872, this in fact being the last award to be made.

The development of the present day coniferous forest in Wootton Courtenay came about after the First World War, when very many wooded areas had been stripped of timber to aid the war effort. The break up of the great estates followed when few landowners could afford to clear and replant and the state controlled Forestry Commission was brought into being.

Meanwhile, farming continued to be the main occupation of the village, providing a much higher level of employment than in today's mechanised agricultural industry. During busy times, such as harvest, men from other village trades would supplement their income by working for local farmers. Often the men would work from 4 am until 10pm or even midnight on a moonlit night. Some farmers would pay two shillings and sixpence or three shillings an hour while others paid the ordinary hourly rate and provided meals." This custom was still in practice until some years after the Second World War. For example, at Brookside Farm, cans of tea (no longer cider) were provided all day, and at teatime large baskets laden with sandwiches, scones, cakes and

Before the refreshing properties of tea were fully appreciated, harvesters refreshed themselves with 'scrumpy' - cider made on the farm - from a 'vurkin' (firkin) such as this.

tarts (always including an extra package for "young Charlie" who ate more than the others) were carried to the fields where the harvesters would rest and chat for a while.

In the days before rabbits were afflicted with mixamatosis they were a useful addition to the food supply and thrived in cornfields. At harvest time when the corn was cut, the rabbits would retreat to the centre of the field as the binder approached. Villagers who owned guns would appear and when the rabbits finally broke cover, the shooting would start. My son can remember how they used to catch the rabbits with their bare hands in the 1950's. On one occasion after the men had taken their rabbits for the pot we were left with more than eighty to dispose of! We had no deep freezers in those days!

In 1920, Wootton Courtenay Estate was said to be about 2,377 acres in size, with the agricultural lands in the valley comprising some of the best in the county. The district was said to be famed for its barley growing, while the higher land provided very useful grazing. Kelly's Directory of Somerset, 1923 records a population in 1911 of 270, the chief crops grown in the Wootton area being wheat, barley and turnips. Though many were still engaged in agriculture, the following list does show an increase in the variety of occupations:-

Poultry Breeder	Frederick May-Brown
Baker	David Burnell
Grocer, draper	
Post Office and	
Boarding House	Mary Burnell*
Motor Repairer	William Burnell
Wheelwright	James Morgan
Blacksmith	William Prescott
Taylor	David De Argués
	Roberts
Mason	Henry Roberts
Poultry Breeder	John Staddon

*The church register of marriages shows that, before 1826, women had no profession

There were 14 farms in the Parish:

Elsworthy	Brockwell
Fairgarden	Ford
Brookside	Manor
Higher Burrow	Middle Burrow
Higher Ranscombe	Lower Ranscombe
Mill	Stile
Wootton Knowle	Huntscott

Farming techniques remained more or less the same for centuries because, until the beginning of the last century, farmers had to rely on basically the same means of power as they had done since the earliest times: that is, man and animal power. It was not until the introduction of the machine on a large scale that farming methods were much altered. Up to this time the old hand tools were almost the same as those used on the farms by the Normans.

During the two world wars, particularly the Second World War, home production of food became essential. Farmers were encouraged to grow more and much land was ploughed for food and corn crops. In order to ensure that this regulation was obeyed, officials employed by the War Agricultural Committee - "men from the war Ag" - visited all farms. At this time of manpower shortage many farmers employed more women on the land, making use of and being very grateful to the girls of the Women's Land Army.

Prisoners of war also worked the land, many being billeted at Crowcombe. Joseph, a German POW, worked at Brookside and Ford Farms and, being a countryman, was an excellent help.

The manpower shortage also probably helped to hasten the use of more and more machinery, thus reducing the number of Wotton Courtenay residents employed in agricultural pursuits. Back in 1971, Bessie Dyke said she visited her old home and had seen "Wootton Courtenay change from a working class community to a refuge for retired people and second homes." Sadly, to those who remember the old days, this is a continuing trend.

Even as early as the 1920's, three of Jack Reed Senior's brothers emigrated to Canada as there was insufficient work on the land for them to farm in Wootton Courtenay

At the end of the 20th Century, much of the farmland listed in Kelly's 1923 directory has been sold. Eight of the farmhouses are now private residences and some of the others are only worked part time. At Fairgarden, Bruce Dascombe and his sons David and Mark rear beef cattle; Michael Reed farms sheep at Higher Ranscombe, and at Riverside Geoffrey and Wendy Vint, Nick and Joanna Webber rear beef cattle and Exmoor Ponies; at Higher Burrow Anthony and Deana Rusher produce beef cattle. At Barleyclose (once part of Brookside Farm), Eve Webber runs a flock of prize Suffolk sheep; Brookside Farm, bought by John Reed at the Estate sale in 1920, was sold in 1990 by his great grandson, Martin Ball, and his wife Caroline since it was no longer possible to maintain a viable dairy farm in the village. They moved to a farm in Cornwall. Alan and Sarah Gooding have converted Lower Ranscombe into a well-established restaurant and, as noted elsewhere, Mill is now a pottery.

Brookside Farm

The 'New' Brookside Farmhouse was built by John Reed in 1923, a few years after the sale of the Estate

Above left: John Reed

Above right: Annie Ball (John Reed's daughter and John Ball's mother) feeding the hens.

Right: Horse –drawn binder in 'Barleyclose'

Until the fifties, Brookside was a typical mixed farm with about 100 sheep, 20 milking cows plus young stock, laying hens, a few geese and a pig to be salted down for the winter. Cereals were grown for the farm stock's concentrate needs

Brookside Farm

Horse drawn mower in Lowertown Meadow

Haymaking: John Ball holds the rake. Reg Court (with the watch chain) worked at Brookside for over 55 years for John Reed, his son-in-law Norman Ball, Norman's son John and John's son Martin. Reg was a champion hedge maker.

John Ball sold milk to the villagers from his horse-drawn cart.

Brookside Farm

Norman Ball and helpers.   Back: Reg Court; Charlie Parsons.
Centre: Nellie?; ? ; George Ball; Trevor Ball?; Dudley Parsons

*John Ball and his
sheep in 1943*

*Haymaking in the late
1940s. Dorothy Ball
drives the Fordson.
John and Norman
strike a pose.*

Brookside
Farm

Harvesting at Brookside
in 1947

Brookside Farm

Left and below:

Threshing at Brookside. The thresher belonged to Fred Case of Withycombe. Fred and Harry Nicholls would do the rounds of the local farms each winter. Labour was pooled between local farms for the task.

In about 1960 the binder and thresher were replaced by the combine harvester

Brookside Farm

A few years after the introduction of the combine harvester the binder, and a specialised thresher were used to cut and thresh wheat from 'Barleyclose' to thatch Highpark. Arch Burgess holds the pitchfork, John Ball is on the load, Peter Ball is driving and Mary Ball is seated bottom left.

John Ball with Peter (left) and Martin feeding sheep in Barleyclose

Feeding the cows in Rackclose, which was at that time rented glebe land. The shed on the left housed laying hens

In the 1960's and 70's John Ball rented the yard at Manor Farm for a flock of laying hens. These buildings have now been converted into holiday cottages.

In the sixties, the cowshed, which had once been a cottage, was still in use and milk was still picked up in churns to go to Rawles Dairies in Minehead.

Above: John Ball milks and fills the churns; Martin waits for milk for his calves.

Right Arch Burgess wheels a churn to the roadside stand. The Shorthorn cows were being replaced by Friesians

Haymaking at Brookside in the mid 60's. Arch Burgess, Martin Ball, Reg Court (driving the tractor) and John Ball

Brookside Farm

Aerial view of Lower Town Wootton Courtenay taken mid 20th Century

By 1970, a milking parlour had been installed in the old cowshed building (paid for by the sale of the land where Cherry Holt and Little Beck bungalows are being built to the left of the picture). A straw yard (top of picture) housed the cows in winter before cubicles were built. The pair of broiler houses (top centre, next to the long thin hen-house) were built in about 1960 to accommodate 3000 broilers.

The farm was sold in 1990. Eddie Bishop and Liz Dunne bought the buildings and have transformed the barn into a dwelling house for themselves and the old cowshed once more accommodates humans, having been converted into holiday cottages suitable for disabled visitors

By the time it was sold, the farm had become specialised in dairying, with over 200 cows being milked. After the sale, some of the land became grazing for beef cattle and sheep; much of it is now used for horses and some is used by Derek Pritchard for his grapevines

Farming in Wootton 'as 'twas'

Haymakers

Fred Crockford, who worked for Miss Lillo Lumb at Riverside (formerly Brookside) Farm

Threshing at Riverside

Take a break: a shooting break (above) or a swig of cider from the firkin (right)

*The pig jib at Manor Farm. Pigs
were laid on the jib after killing to
be cleaned and scraped. As can be
seen, it had other uses!*

*Jack Reed Snr
shearing sheep*

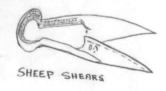

SHEEP SHEARS

Cutcombe and District Young Farmers' Club

Stock judging at Cutcombe Auction Field.
Entrants include:
Henry Stevens (West Harwood, Weddon Cross - 7th from l), John Ball (9th), Olive Dascombe (nee Stevens - 12th);Gwen Burnell (nee Thorne, Fairgarden Farm - 14th). The Dascombes farmed Fairgarden after the Thornes and Gwen's husband Jack.

On the left are Gwen Burnell and Henry Stevens

Cutcombe and District Young Farmers' Club

George Ball and Jack Reed returning calves which they had reared for twelve months to be judged and auctioned. John Ball and his entry are to the left of the horse.

John Ball (front right) acted as a stock judge for the Young farmers' Cub. This was at Minehead Auction, near the station. The site has now become a car park.

Transport

The lane that runs up beside the village hall and over North Hill (not to be confused with the North Hill overlooking Minehead!) used to be the main route to Minehead. "New Road", was upgraded and became the public road from Wootton Courtenay to Porlock and Minehead. It has a corner overlooking Porlock Vale, which can still be tricky. In the early 1900's the first two car owners in the village (both ladies, but that is by-the-way!) collided at that point. About 50 years later another local character, Tommy Roberts, who had sported L plates on his moped for many years, fell off at the same spot. "Aw, that offen 'appens", he explained.

The first bus to run from Wootton Courtenay was operated by William Prescott of Luccombe in the early 1920s. He used a Daimler which could be adapted for use as a lorry or fitted with seats to carry passengers.

Later, William Burnell (listed in Kelly's 1923 directory as a motor engineer) started another service from Wootton. It ran for many years to and from Minehead via Timberscombe and Dunster. By 1930 the Wootton - Minehead service was the only one he ran.

Work being carried out on 'New Road' in the 1930's

Motorised public transport came to Wootton when William Burnell started a service in 1919 when he came out of the army. At first, passengers were carried to and from Minehead in the sidecar attached to his motor cycle. He later bought a Maxwell car before converting to motor buses, running weekly market services from Kings Brompton to Taunton and Minehead.

For a while 'Bill' Burnell and Geoff Pugsley of Wheddon Cross were in partnership, but soon the business was split with Geoff running the cattle haulage side and Bill running the garage and buses. Apparently he was also able to take advantage of the growing tourist industry, picking up holiday visitors from Minehead on the 3 pm bus, taking them to Venniford or Wootton Courtenay for a walk followed by tea at the Dunkery Beacon Hotel or one of the tea gardens before catching the bus back to town.

In 1933, Mrs Morgan of Woodbine Cottage, we are told, broke her leg and wished to visit her son in Brighton. William removed some seats from his bus and took her in her wheelchair to Brighton, promising that if she died he would bring her back. When this occurred he drove to Brighton again and a plan was made to load the coffin into the bus before folk were about. However, to everyone's consternation, just as they were putting the coffin into the bus, the early morning detachment of police marched by!

The service's busiest period was during and just after the second world war when it ran twice daily (Wednesdays and Sundays excepted).

At one time ice was brought in the bus from Luttrell's sawmills to Mr Rook, who owned the Wootton Courtenay stores, and to Miss Floyd at Timberscombe. She made wonderful ice cream in a bucket with a handle which she (and volunteers such as young John Ball) turned by hand. The bus was also greatly valued as a parcel service, especially during the war when petrol was rationed. Goods were brought, for example, from MacFisheries and Batchelors the grocers at a charge of 4d each. During the war, when there were evacuees living in the district, the bus often returned to Dunster to pick up a second load of passengers. The bus was also used by the local Home Guard during the war.

The bus has also been used over the years since 1930 to transport schoolchildren to secondary school in Minehead, or to meet the Western National (now First) buses at Venniford. After the Second World War, when Wootton Courtenay School closed, free transport was provided for primary school children to Timberscombe School. At first this was provided by cars. Peter Ball can remember being driven by Mr or Mrs Bower in a Rolls Royce shooting break. This service was taken over by taxis, and subsequently buses, run by William Burnell's son George.

The first bus used in the school run was a World War II utility bus, which at one stage also took secondary school pupils from Wootton and Luccombe to Venniford. On Thursdays, it also operated as the service bus, which by that time only operated on that day of the week.

In the 50s and 60s, many people - mainly housewives - used the Thursday bus for weekly shopping trips. They often took the opportunity to meet for a drink in a Minehead cafe. Gwenny Burnell obviously thought this was acting above their station. "What do 'ee think,?" she asked us one day, "They there Witten wimmin, in there drinkin coffee. Ooever do em think they be?"

The school and public services have been run by a number of operators over the years, with the public service more often than not still restricted to a Thursday. The school bus is now run by Somerset County Council and the public service by First.

George Burnell still opens the garage for repairs and 'information exchange', but no longer runs buses or sells petrol.

Above: Part of Burnells' fleet in about 1930, including a 14 seater Chevrolet (left) and a Bedford (right)

Left:

George and Rosemary (William Burnell's Children) in a 1941 Austin Seven given to George for his 10th birthday

Below:

William Burnell's Maxwell taxi in about 1928. The apex of the village hut - subsequently the village hall kitchen, can be seen in the centre background.

Chapter Nine

Iron Mining

In 1839 the Director of the Ordnance Geological Survey, Sir Henry de la Beche FRS issued a report on "The Geology of Cornwall, Devon and West Somerset." Included is the information that: - "The mass of the Exmoor country is ill supplied with lime" but "in the gulf occupied by the red sandstone series from Porlock by Holnicote, Luckham and Wootton Courtenay, towards Timberscome we again find a lime conglomerate with a magnesic-calcareous cement in sufficient quantity to make the rock worth working for lime, running from Doverhay by Luckham to Huntsgate and two patches at Well and Knoll Farms."

In the Wootton Courtenay Somerset Valuation list for 1864, among the fields rented to John Copp of Ramscombe Farm is listed a piece of land on which there is a "quarry, lime kiln and waste". In the garden of a house now called Quarry Field in Ranscome Road are the remains of a lime kiln where lime was brought to be burnt and used on the land as fertilizer.

In 1830 James Savage wrote that sea pebbles were washed up by the strong tides from the Welsh coast and that "great quantities were burnt into lime which is the principal manure used by farmers in this area." Much limestone was also brought from Wales in its natural state and burned here with charcoal to produce fertilizer.

During the mid 19th Century there seems to have been a good deal of trading with small ships to and from Wales and along the English coast. Jan Ridler's grandfather not only farmed in the district but also built up a considerable business as a timber and general merchant. "One of his own little coasting vessels would fetch bark from Porlock Weir, ballasted with bricks made there, and carry it to Boscastle in Cornwall and return with slate from Delabole Quarry, about the best available and much longer lasting than the local Treborough slate." "My father," Jan said "had Tom Court's house and the next one roofed with Delabole slate in 1862." These two cottages, now known as Appledore are in Lower Town. From the geological survey we learn that "The Delabole quarries have long been celebrated for producing a beautiful and durable material, combining considerable lightness with strength." (1758).

Sir Henry de la Beche's report continues: - "The lower portion of the series (of red sandstone from Porlock towards Timberscombe) is also remarkable for the presence of red hematitic iron ore in such quantities that it is in some localities worked in the manner of a quarry .... This ore is to be found at Brockwell." Brockwell was already in production for, on 6th April, 1836, the Taunton Courier reported that "Mr Crawshay the great iron master is working with a good deal of vigour the recently discovered mine at Wootton Courtenay which affords employment to the poor of the neighbourhood. The farmers are also enabled to turn their teams to good account and poor men with their donkeys are likewise engaged in hauling the ore to Minehead where it is shipped to Wales." Mr John Reed in 1930 recalled that he and his father used to haul iron ore from the iron mines in the Quarme valley.

The report continues: - "Sometimes more than a hundred carriages of various descriptions may be observed on the roads leading to the ports." (Minehead and Porlock Weir). "The ladies, however, and singularly enough, the young ladies, residing in the town are most annoyed and complain very loudly at being disturbed at so early an hour in the morning by the noise of the vehicles."

On one occasion when the rector of Selworthy walked to Wootton Courtenay rectory to call on Mr Scott, he commented "The dust on the road from the Iron Ore carts is very troublesome."

"It should be noted, perhaps, that John Fourney Luttrell Esq. Of Dunster Castle, although entitled to Quay Dues (in Minehead) at the rate of 5d per ton on the ore shipped, has, with his accustomed liberality in order to encourage the trade of the port consented to accept a mere acknowledgement only."

An extract from the Wootton Courtenay church register in 1872 reads:-

Marriage:

G. Bryant – miner, Old Cleeve
Mary Ann Gould – spinster,
                    Wootton Courtenay

Perhaps G. Bryant was a miner from Wales as Mr Crawshay owned mines at Merthyr Tydfil and Welsh miners are known to have worked in the Somerset mines.

It has been suggested that the present farmhouse at Higher Brockwell, recently sold at a high price as an "old farmhouse", was in fact originally built as a row of miners' cottages.

Evidence of the mines is still visible on the edge of the moor between Brockwell and Ford. The location is known locally as "Iron Pits" and Woodcock Lane is the old track along which ore was taken to Porlock Weir for shipment to Wales.

Ironpits in 2007

There were evidently deep mines as well as surface workings. A tractor in Highpark, part of Brookside Farm adjoining the moor at Ironpits, fell into a hole which was reckoned to be the remains of an air shaft.

As shown in the 1929 entry of the Parish Meeting Records, Mrs Hughes, who then owned the land, allowed one of the old iron pits to be used as a dump for unburnable rubbish, in conjunction with the "Jug and Bottle" service.

The remains of the old rubbish dump at 'Ironpits

A bottle found at the site of the Ironpits rubbish dump

Some years later Mrs Hughes gave this part of the moor to the National Trust. It is hoped that now in the 21st Century those responsible for its maintenance will remember that the beauty of the heather on the moor can only be managed by man.

Heather survives by the scrub land being burnt. Swaling, as it is called, must be completed by the end of March, leaving grazing for sheep and cattle, without which the heather will vanish to be replaced with gorse and the poisonous and rapidly spreading bracken.

Moorland around Ironpits in 2007

Chapter 10

Houses

Wootton Courtenay does not appear to have been at any time a large settlement area, most of the inhabitants living in surrounding farms and cottages, with two main groups of houses in Higher Town near the church and at Lower Town near the River Hanney at the bottom of the hill known as "Lower Town Steep".

Today, in both areas, the number of dwellings has increased, mainly by infilling along the roads, much of this occurring between the two world wars at a time of much agricultural depression. Now, in addition to National Park controls, there is a conservation order in certain areas to control any proposed development.

Highertown (above) and Lowertown (below) in the early 20th Century

The bottom of Lowertown Steep with Annie Ferris, circa 1929 (above) and Dorothy Ball with her mother, Gladys Powell in the 1960's (right)

In Higher Town, one of the oldest buildings is possibly the Rectory, built circa 1500 when it consisted of a hall open to the roof with lateral fireplace, buttery and two parlours with a chamber over. A kitchen and brewhouse, with malt and grain store were built away from the house.

Of course, many alterations have been made over the years and it is now a pleasant, privately owned, modern residence.

The Old Rectory in the early (above) and late (left) twentieth century

The house to the right of the Church Steps, in the year 2000 known as Manor House (Wootton Courtenay has never had a manor house, as there has never been a resident Land Lord) in an early survey was listed as "Churcheys". A fine silver flagon, dated 1641, in the possession of the church was the gift of George Churchey who also left ten pounds to the poor of Luccombe. The inscription on the flagon reads:- "Wootton Courtenay donum Georgii Churchey".

Above: the external appearance of 'Manor House' has changed little in the half century or so since this picture was taken.

Below: The adjoining Manor Farm

He may have died just before 1641 as his widow Anne is assessed at 9s 9d and her name appears in the Lay Subsidy Rolls for that year. His daughter Joan was baptized in 1607 and Elizabeth in 1609. In the house today are examples of old beams and rafters.

Jasmine Cottage

On the left of Church Steps, Jasmine Cottage is on the site of the old Poor House. In 1864 it was listed as the 'Late Poor House', consisting of five cottages, occupied by Wm Burnell and John Roberts and owned by William England and New Cottage owned by Wm England and W Burnell, occupied by Wm Burgess, George Court and W Burnell

Annie Palmer, who died in the early 1940s remembered when her Uncle lived in the cottage and they baked bread in an oven in the churchyard wall, probably using peat. In an 1842 survey a malt house and a peat house, tenanted by a Robert Price, were listed and in her memories of the year 1900 Bessie Dyke recalled how peat was used for nearly all heating and cooking and described how her father cut the turfs, piled them in large mounds, put a stone on them on which he wrote his initials and fetched them home when they were dry in a horse and putt.

In the early 1900s part of the adjoining property was owned by Mr George Burnell, a tailor, who employed up to 6 men as tailors who worked in the room above the shop. In recent years, buttons and other items have been found under the floorboards. George would travel by horse and trap to Porlock, and as far as Lynmouth, to meet customers - probably mainly hunting people - to collect orders for suits, coats, breeches etc. and when the orders were completed by his tailors, would make another day's excursion to deliver the finished articles.

In later years his son ran a garage, car repair shop and bus service from the premises. His grandson inherited and enlarged the business and still lives in the house there, next to the garage. An old photograph suggests that this was the site of the original shop, which was burnt down shortly after 1916.

George's wife ran a general store. In 1923 Kelly's Directory of Somerset lists "Mrs Mary Burnell – Grocer, Draper and Post Office, in that part of the building which is still the village shop with living quarters above.

George Burnell (left) with his tailors Fred Date, Dave Roberts, Norman Ball, Walter Copp, William Quick and B Bowditch.

George Burnell's premises (right) and one of his advertisements from the Minehead and Porlock Vale Magazine in 1889 (below)

GEORGE BURNELL,

TAILOR, DRAPER,

General Commission Agent, &c.

GENERAL WAREHOUSE, WOOTTON COURTENAY.

FAMILY MOURNING.

Agent for Bradbury's and Wheeler & Wilson's Sewing Machines; Jones & Co.'s Bristol Organs and Harmoniums, and other best Makers; Breech-loading Guns by best Makers; United Kingdom, Temperance, and General Insurance Office; all kinds of Agricultural Implements, Hearth Ovens, Pumps, &c., manufactured by Dening & Co., Chard; Simpson's Calf Meal and Spice.

Specialities in Tailoring; Gent.'s Suits and Hunting Outfits; Ladies' Riding Habits, Covert Coats, and Costumes; Youths' and Boys' Suits. A competent staff of Men. New Patterns. Fair Charges.

Five of the tailors outside the shop in 1906

Mary Burnell's general store

Part of the building was destroyed when Mr and Mrs Jack Reed lived here shortly after their marriage in 1916. The section with the awning is now a garage for the shop and the cottage has been replaced with George Burnell's house and garage.

A small garage (to the right of the cars) was built after the fire. It was in turn replaced by the current premises.

Over the years there have been many changes of ownership of the shop until, in 1990, the owners decided to sell not only the business, but also the property and it was feared the shop would be closed. However, due to the magnificent efforts and enthusiasm of a few villagers, enough money was raised to buy the property. Many problems were finally overcome and in 1991 the "Wootton Courtenay Villagers' Stores was opened by the then local MP and Minister for Defence, Tom King.

It is a private limited company owned and controlled by the villagers, the stores and house being leased to tenants on terms giving them an incentive to provide a good service and the possibility of earning a reasonable living.

Fernlea. (below) Access to the stairs leading to the first floor can be seen at the bottom left of the photo

Thus, in 2003 Wootton Courtenay is one of the few remaining English villages to have its own village store, much appreciated as the centre for news and gossip and the service it provides.

Opposite the shop is Fernlea, a house built on the site of an old cottage by George Burnell in the 1860s. The land was leased to be used for a dwelling house or coffee tavern. In the late 1890s, George, who was a strict temperance man, wanted to provide an alternative to the temptations of the recently built Dunkery Hotel, and hence he built steps up to the first floor of the house where men could go and drink coffee and have a game of dominoes. The premises were sold in 1934 and used as tea rooms and grocery store. At one stage subsequently the then occupants suspected that a poltergeist was at work, and an exorcism was carried out! Now it is a private house.

Next door to the garage is Pound Cottage. Behind this was the village pound in the days when an enclosed area was provided for stray ponies from the moor, and wandering sheep, which were confined until a fine was paid. Then they were allowed through the gate of which, so we are told, one of the posts is still standing.

Pound Cottage appears at one time to have been used as a non-conformist chapel. Phoebe Quick, Bill Farmer and Bessie Dyke – all members of families who had lived in Wootton Courtenay for many years, remembered their mothers telling them that Pound Cottage was once used as a chapel and that they had been to services there.

It was interesting to read an article by John Glynn in the 2003 Edition of 'Exmoor' telling the story of the Exmoor Bible Christians. In the early 1800s travelling ministers - men and women – walked many miles over Exmoor preaching either in the open air or wherever a room could be found. Gradually, in many villages, chapels were built for the Wesleyan, Methodist, Baptist and other independent meetings. However, in some villages, Wootton Courtenay among them, services were held for many years in cottages and farmhouses.

Highertown about a century ago, with Pound Cottage on the left

In the 1960s the Jury family lived at Pound Cottage. Stan was Mr Docker's chauffeur and is seen here with the pre-selector gearbox Daimler limousine which he was not allowed to drive too fast! Arriving at Taunton Station one snowy day he observed that "E could uv rode 'is bloody pooshbike an' got yer quicker."

Adjoining Pound Cottage is the present Stag Cottage, recorded in the 1861 census return as the Rose and Crown, an inn, with Thomas Knight as the innkeeper. In 1881 a notice of sale read as follows:- "For Sale. The fully licensed Rose and Crown Inn and six cottages adjoining."

The house was later called Rosemount and apparently the Knight family continued to live there.

Highertown, at the turn of the century with Rosemount (formerly the Rose and Crown Inn) to the left of the picture ,

Rosemount as a tea-room in the 1920s

In the late 1930s Mrs Knight ran the house as a temperance hotel (a change from when it was the 'Rose and Crown'!). She also provided teas for hikers (see Chapter 13) . The house looks much the same today. It is now known as Stag Cottage.

George Burnell's aunt, Mrs Slade, was at that time running a tea garden at Fernlea,, which had been home to her father's coffee house.

Wreford

Approximately 1900

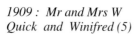

1909 : Mr and Mrs W Quick and Winifred (5)

The building was enlarged and the thatch replaced with tiles some time before the estate sale in 1920. For many years 'Buster' and Joy May-Brown sold the produce from his market garden from a shop in the garage of the house

The Eastern end of the building is now a separate dwelling known as Peartree Cottage

At the entrance to the Playing Field where Butts Lane meets Brockwell Lane are two bungalows built in the early 20th century, known as Butts Orchard, named after butts or archery targets. Bows and arrows were used in archery practice, which was officially encouraged, and a legal requirement for men from Saxon until Tudor times. It is appropriate to note that in 2004 an archery club is using the village playing field for regular practice. Times have changed! This is for pleasure and not, as in the past, preparation for war. We know that during the 16th century parishes were responsible for providing men prepared to defend the country.

In 1584 there is a record announcing the sailing of a large Spanish fleet and orders were given for putting men in readiness for the defence of the sea coast. Somerset was charged to supply the maritime counties and the inhabitants to be "brought up and exercised in the use of the long bowe etc." This must have been the site (i.e. "The Butts") where the archers exercised in Wootton parish. During the 1920s one of the Butts Orchard houses was bought by the Nursing Association as a home for the District Nurse.

Butts Orchard in 2007

Alvestoke, on Brockwell Road, was built for Mr Gibbs, the headmaster of Minehead Grammar School (formerly the County School) between the two world wars

Higher Brockwell, on the edge of the moor between Wootton and Ford was recently sold as "an old farmhouse" for a very high price but there is no doubt that it was originally built as miners' cottages to serve the nearby Iron Pits.

Nearby Brockwell may have been built as a miner's house, but was a farmhouse for many years. George and May Reed farmed there in the early 1900s. Later, Mrs Barbara Binnie was renowned for the Welsh Ponies which she bred there. Her son and his wife still live at Brockwell.

Brockwell in the 1900s (left) George Reed (above, and with May, above left) was farming there. Externally, the house has changed very little (below)

In the 1930s, Douglas Lang helped George Reed at Brockwell after school each day. Tommy Vaulter was the full time employee. Douglas remembers the horse, "Nelson" He had been a timber horse, which explained why he was always very reluctant to continue working after 4.30 in the afternoon!

At one time, before the land was farmed, Alfie and Annie Court lived at Brockwell and the tale is told of an occasion when Annie went shopping to Minehead, walking up "Old Road Way" (the old road to Minehead) up over Wootton North Hill and down through the suburbs of Minehead – a round walk of about twelve miles. To her dismay, when she arrived home, she found that she had not done the shopping her husband had wanted. Rather than face his wrath (he was a "real old devil"), she walked straight back to Minehead for the goods.

Alfie (left) and Annie (above) Court

A similar tale was told in the Free Press of the servant girl 'Susan':-

We have all heard that in the old days most people remained in the parish in which they were born and had no occasion to travel outside. Of course, it just is not true. They went out for work and into service.

Still, it is doubtful whether many travelled so far and so fast and came so quickly home again as the servant girl from Wootton Courtenay who went to buy "barm" for her "Missus".

It was May or June 1833. Her name is not known, but since she does not deserve to be without one, let us call her Susan. A farmer's wife of Wootton Courtenay sent her apprentice girl, our Susan, to Minehead for barm, and as she particularly needed it for brewing she ordered her to "be sure and not come back without it". Susan searched "from one end o' Minyard to tuther" without success. But just as she was leaving the Queen's Head on the quay a party of ladies also came out to take the ship for Wales. Susan, being either conscientious or in mortal fear of returning to her "Missus" barmless and inconsolate, also took her seat in the boat.

The sailors thought she belonged to the passengers, the passengers the opposite. Half way across they discovered their mistake, and Susan told them "Missus told her not to come back without the barm, and as she would not find any in Minyard, she was going to Wales for it".

A fair wind and tide carried the boat over in two hours. The sailors, entering into the spirit of the thing, sent her to a public house where she bought the barm. They then "bout ship for Minehead, crossed in three hours and put Susan ashore." When she reached Wootton, "Missus" began scolding her for taking so long over a two or three-hour trip to Minehead.

Susan persisted in her story, a messenger was sent to the town and found, to his amazement, that she had told the truth and had been from Wootton over to Wales and home again, all between breakfast and tea time.

On Ranscombe Road, where the modern bungalow "Greencombe" now stands there were for many years a house and buildings known as Hurfords. In 1532 there is a reference in a book "Well's Wills", by Rev. F.W. Weaver, to the will of Roger Hurford, who lived here. Until around the 1950s this was a bakehouse and shop, the last baker to produce and sell bread in the village being David Burnell and his assistant "Sonny" carter.

The old bakehouse and shop as it was until the 1950s (right).

In the 1960s the building was demolished, revealing old beams and an upstairs fireplace (below)

Bessie Dyke remembered how, in the early 1900's, "Burnell the baker heated ovens with wood and baked, not only bread, but also dough cakes, cut rounds (a kind of plain scone) and <u>real</u> hot cross buns. To earn a few pence at Easter Time, lads would load large baskets with them and take them round to farms and hamlets. The baker would also, for a few pence, cook the cottagers' Sunday lunches. His sons Wynham and David took bread to all the villagers, going as far as Porlock Wier."

David carried on the business and is still remembered for selling off cheaply tins of food which had lost their labels – literally a lucky dip! Douglas Lang remembers going to buy a tin of pineapple for his mother. "I think that must be two for one" says Dave, giving him two tins - one of which did contain pineapple - and charging him for one. Dave also sold groceries and postage stamps. It was not unknown for bacon rashers and stamps to be found on the same counter, obviously having received visits from the mice. Douglas said there were often mice to be seen running among the provisions, but Dave acted the innocent: "Coo, I think I've got a bally mouse 'ere." Nevertheless, it was always a pleasure to shop at Dave's and have bread delivered to the door by Sonny.

Ranscombe

Ranscombe, with Timberscombe in the background

Higher Ranscombe Farmhouse

Ranscombe

*Lower Ranscombe, now
a restaurant*

*In the 1940s Higher Ranscombe's mixed
farming enterprise was typical of the area
and included a small herd of milking Short-
horns*

*The cottage between Lower and Higher Ranscombe - next to
Ranscombe Farm buildings - is now known as 'The Creeks' and the
thatch has been replaced by slates.*

Down the hill known as Lower Town Steep, is Orchard House, built in the early 1900s by Edward Reed as a house to retire to back in his home village when he left the police force in Street.

He called it "Restholme."

It was greatly extended after Mrs Docker bought it and her son Noel continued to live there until his death. It has now been converted into flats.

Orchard House

Bishops Cottages on the right

At the bottom of the hill in Lower Town, a row of cottages known as Bishops Cottages are examples of houses built with chimneys towards the street. During the Civil War 1642 – 1646 in the reign of Charles I, many houses were built in this way and tradition says it was common in this and other parts of Somerset and adopted for the purpose of protecting the inhabitants from the prying eyes and secret attacks of evilly disposed persons of an opposite party.

In the West of England many houses were built of rough stones and "cob" – a composition of clay and reed well mixed together and the wall made smooth on the surface after the mixture had dried. During the early 1900s one of the rooms in No. 4 Bishops Cottages was used by

4, Bishops Cottages

shoemakers. One of them was Abe Hill, described thus by Betty Dyke:- "The shoemaker was Abe Hill. My parents said for those days he had a good education, sent out his bills every quarter, written in perfect copper plate and he must have used some sort of filing system, every item being written in this way: - "a pair of working boots for John, 12/6d." He lived in squalor and, to quote my father "lived like a pig, and died like a dog." He was more often drunk than sober, but was a wonderful craftsman. His boots were all hand sewn and would last, even with hard wear, for two years." He was succeeded by John Reed, who later farmed at Riverside and Brookside.

The lane to Riverside Farm was in the past known as Duck Street, which may refer to a ducking pond where suspected witches used to be ducked. It could also be named for the fact that ducks could be seen swimming in the River Hanny, beside which the road runs. Wheddons, at the top of Duck Street, must have taken its name from John Wheddon, who was recorded in the Hearth Tax returns for 1664-5.

Riverside Cottage in Duck Street

The pair of cottages on the right is now the dwelling known as Appledore. The door leading onto the street is for 'Allens' or 'Tom's House'

On the opposite side of the road is a dwelling called 'Appledore'. This originally consisted of two cottages, with a common roof composed of Delabole Slate, brought from Cornwall in John Ridler's grandfather's coasting vessel.The lower of the two cottages was previously called 'Allens', but for many years after World War II it was known by local people as "Tom's House".

In 1921 it was let on a weekly tenancy to Mr Thos Court, at a rental of 1s 4d per week.

His son Tom, a well-known and much respected character, lived there until he died in 1985. Tom was a tailor before the war, but returned to become a gardener and was very involved in every village activity. You name it, Tom was there helping. He was known throughout the district for his rendering of the "Jan Stewer" yarns at entertainments and social events.

On the other side of Butts' Lane – a bridle path leading to Brockwell Lane – are two cottages now called Vine Cottage and Woodbine Cottage which were described in the Estate Sale Catalogue in 1921 as "A terrace, comprising a pair of cottages and business premises" and were sold to John Reed for £300.

Tom Court with his mother (centre) and Annie Ball

Included in Vine Cottage was "a large and well lighted Tailor's workshop" and the property was let to Mr D Roberts for this purpose at £7 per annum. Dave later transferred his business to the cottage in Higher Town now known as "Finch", which was later occupied by the widow of E.W. Hendy, the author of "Somerset Birds". One of the Ball family's treasured possessions is a tailored coat made by one of Dave's tailors for John Ball's grandmother.

Vine Cottage as a tailors workshop in the 1920's (above)

Vine Cottage is now a private dwelling (above)

The business later transferred to Finch Cottage (left)

Woodbine Cottage next door, was previously known as Myrtle Cottage. In the 1921 sale catalogue it had a yard, Carpenter's shop, open shed, pigstye and closet and was let to Mr J Morgan at £6. 10s per annum. In 1923 he was listed as a wheelwright.

During World War II Mrs Munnings, wife of Alfred (later Sir Alfred) Munnings, bought the cottage and changed its name from Myrtle to Woodbine in memory of one of her horses*. Alfred decided to store some of his paintings there and once again some of the seats in Burnell's bus were removed by the driver, Dudley Parsons, who recalls how he drove with Mrs Munnings to London, Mr Munnings driving his own car. They spent the night in their London house with bombs falling in the neighbourhood and ceilings coming down. Supper consisted of a tin of pilchards, followed by tinned rice, the plates being wiped clean with newspaper. The following day, Dudley drove the bus home, loaded with most of the valuable paintings.

Alfred did not live here, but in his house at Withypool, where he spent his time walking, riding over the moor and painting.

Gwen Burnell lived in Wootton Courtenay for many years after her parents, Mr and Mrs Thorne bought Fairgarden Farm in the 1920s. She told me that she remembered Mrs Munnings when she lived at Woodbine Cottage during the war and kept her horses nearby.

She was a smart lady who used to ride sidesaddle and Gwen remembered how she would often ride up to Fairgarden with sugar and tea which she offered to Mrs Thorne in exchange for butter and cream (of which there was no shortage on the farm). When Alfred came to Wootton Courtenay he "looked like an old tramp in a dirty old smock." I don't think Gwen thought much of his paintings when her family were invited to see them and were offered one at, I think she said, five pounds, but they couldn't afford it. She "didn't think it was worth a damn", but she wished she had had it in later years!

Mr and Mrs Morgan (above) and with their family outside Myrtle Cottage (right)

---

* Sir Alfred, in one of his books, says that his wife "bought a Cottage in Wootton Courtenay "for a mere song". This was from John Ball's grandfather, John Reed

Forge Cottage next door was, for many years, the village blacksmith's workplace and residence. It was described in the 1921 brochure as "a well built Smithy with forge, cottage and small yard and was sold to the tenant, Mr W Priscott, for £280. The last smiths to shoe horses there were Fred Kent and his son John. Fred was a well known and loved Exmoor character who actually lived in Porlock. It was another sign of the change in village life when John closed the forge and travelled round the district with his horse shoeing equipment in a motor van.

A thatched cottage on the bank of the river Hanney beside the bridge is now called Bridge Cottage and was previously known as Rawles Cottage. It was at one time a public house or, possibly, Ale House - "The Rising Sun". In 1842 this was listed under the name of Thomas Baker. A wine jar dating from about 1715 and a quantity of broken clay "churchwardens' pipes" were dug up in a field behind the cottage.

It is known that there were several mills, worked by water wheels, between Dunster and Wootton Courtenay and I wonder if this could have been one of them.

The Forge in the 1940s

Bridge Cottage, which was previously known as Rawles Cottage and had once been 'The Rising Sun'.

An early 18th century wine bottle (above) and the bowls of 18th and 19th century churchwardens' pipes (below) found in the field across the river behind the cottage

"Crockfords", reached by a little footbridge over the River Hanney, was originally three thatched cottages.

Both Crockfords and Bridge Cottage contain examples of ancient beams and joints.

'Crockfords' was once three thatched cottages (above, below and left)

The thatch has been replaced and the building forms a single modern dwelling (left)

Lt Col O.B.G. Philby (cousin of the spy, Kim Philby) and his family lived in Crockfords for many years. His daughter, Eve Webber, still lives in a neighbouring modern bungalow

Over the bridge on the Burrow Road is High Park Cottage, sold at the estate sale as "a pair of well placed semi-detached cottages with garden, with outside – outhouses, stone and tiled pigstyes and closets, water supply at a tap outside each door" In the boundary wall there are still the remains of a well.

In 1864 this cottage was listed as Reives Cottage. I would like to think that this is a mis-spelling of "Reeves", a reeve being a minor official or manorial supervisor of villeins (feudal serfs or tenants entirely subject to a lord or attached to a manor).

A reeve would collect rents and taxes and have been responsible for the repair of roads and bridges as well as overseeing service in the time of war. Wootton Courtenay always had an absentee landlord so this could have been his reeve or agent's dwelling house.

There is evidence of it having being built (in two stages) around or before 1700. It is now a grade II listed building.

The outside closets, which existed until the 1970s, had been earth closets. The contents of these, plus ashes from the open fireplaces, no doubt contributed to the dark, rich nature of the soil cultivated to good purpose by John Ball after his retirement from farming.

High Park

On the outskirts of the village at Burrow, Lower Burrow Farm House has, like Orchard House, been converted into holiday flats. The land here must have been farmed for many centuries as, in 1941, the barn became the first example of the jointed "crutch" type to be discovered and probably dates from around 1500.

At Elsworthy, where Stile road ends and the lane to Spangate begins, there is a fine modern house, Annicombe, on the edge of Exmoor with wonderful views. During the 1930's the house which stood there was burnt to the ground, and a rumour was spread about that jewellery and valuables were buried under the ashes. Apparently, although several hopefuls spent time searching, nothing was ever discovered.

In 1929 an article in the Evening Standard reported that Wootton Courtenay had solved the servant problem by "employing men and boys for household work. Masters and mistresses, it is said, find them much more satisfactory than the 'flighty giddy pated' maids of all work whose places they have taken." In the year 2000 an elderly resident remembered when two pit boys from the mining district of Spennymoor, Durham were employed as cook and parlourmaid at Annicombe

There must have been a change of heart in the village since, as we read previously, the Parish Council in 1929 had said that the people of Wootton Courtenay "could offer no house-accommodation or employment at present".

One of the boys married a local girl and his family lived in the area for many years.

Annicombe House after the fire

Chapter Eleven

The Church

The oldest parts of the existing church, dedicated to All Saints, are the eastern end of the Chancel and lower part of the tower which probably date from about 1250. They may have formed part of a complete earlier Norman church, as there is a record that the Norman owner of the Manor of Wootton gave the church to a small French priory then being founded at Stogursey. The Church is not recorded in the Doomesday records since at that time churches paid no taxes.

The living is rectoral and in 1292 was valued at 7 marks, 3 shillings and 4 pence. A century before Henry VIII had confiscated abbeys and priories for his own benefit, Henry VI had dissolved some small "alien priories" and used the proceeds to found centres of education.

The proceeds from the dissolution of Stogursey were used to found an educational centre at Eton. The Provost and Fellows of Eton College thus became patrons who appoint the rectors of Wootton.

The church contains examples of the best work done in the perpendicular period, especially in its windows and roof carvings, as well as other unusual ancient features. A blocked recess to the left of the chancel arch was once a "squint", which enabled people standing in the North Aisle to see the Alter at the east end of the chancel. Also of interest are the external window moulds and niches for statues on two of the nave pillars.

The Nave was rebuilt in 1450, when the North Aisle was added, the roofs of both being fine examples of the West Country "Wagon Roof" style.

A distinctive feature of the church, and a prominent local landmark, is the "saddleback" top of the tower, which replaced the previous battlements and now houses the bells.

The church in 1839 (above) and with the distinctive saddleback tower from victorian times (right)

The bells are inscribed:

1. Given in 1903 by Thomas Burnell.
                Weight 5cwts

2. Walter Court
    Thomas Gillam   Wardens
                    T/W 1710

3. God save the Church

    Walter Court
    Thomas Gillam   Wardens
                    T/W 1710

4. Recast by John Warne & Sons
                London 1876

5. Campana vivas convocated eccleseii
                    1606

6. Tenor:
    Andrew Bryant
    Wm. Berryman
                Wardens
                T/P 1629
                Weight 13 Cwts

Wootton Courtenay has traditionally been proud of its fine ringing teams. Plaques in the tower commemorate a number of historic 'rings'. On new Year's Eve the bells were muffled to alternate the six normal rings for the New Year with six almost inaudible for the old. Afterwards, the ringers would meet at Brookside for a celebratory drink.

The ringers association with Miss Stanley, the Rector's sister, in the 1920's

The church has a very fine carved oak rood screen. The following information is from a notice in the church:

Towards the end of the nineteenth century a Mr Pennington held carving classes locally. This was encouraged by Sir Thomas Dyke Acland and Wootton's rector, the Rev. E.P. Stanley. Parishioners attended classes in a room in the Rectory and produced some excellent carving and in particular the carving which fills the tower arch followed by a very fine screen in the chancel arch which, in 1921, was dedicated to the memory of Rev. Stanley's wife.
The names of the people who worked on the carving in the church are, in many cases, an echo of the names of people still living locally.

Mr and Mrs N Ball

Mrs G Burnell

Mr W Conibere

Mr W Copp

Mr G Eames

Mrs Floyd

Mrs G Gooding

Mrs F Adams

Mr C.G. Payne

Mr and Mrs G Reed

Miss H Reed

The interior of All Saints' Church, Wootton Courtenay, showing the chancel screen carved by local residents and dedicated in 1921

The first entry in the church register dates from 1558.

A 1584 entry tells us that the sailing of a large Spanish fleet was announced and orders given for putting men in readiness for the defence of the sea coast. Somerset was charged to supply the maritime counties and the inhabitants to "Be brought up and exercised in the use of the long bowe etc".

The bishops were "to take order" with the clergy, either to furnish light horse or to compound at the rate of £25 for each horse charge. It is recorded that the parson of Wootton Courtenay paid £65.0.0.

During the war between the Roundheads and the Puritans, Wootton people became involved in national events through their Loyalist rector, John Morley. In the floor of the church nave there is a well lettered stone naming two sons of John Morley, Rector of Wootton and prebendary of Timberscombe, and also Vicar of North Petherton, where there is a fine brass to his wife. Walker's "Sufferings of the Clergy" says "He was likewise plundered, his sons were imprisoned and he was forced to compound for his temporals. He lived to be restored and died at North Petherton in 1661 leaving behind him the character of a good and pious man".

Although Morley was a Royalist, he made voluntary contributions to Parliamentary funds during the civil war in order, no doubt, to keep out of trouble. He returned to the king's side when the Royal Army returned to the county. This may have a bearing on the complaint of Charles Steynings of Holnicote when Cromwell, in 1648, billeted a troop of horse in the parishes of Minehead, Luccombe, Selworthy, Timberscombe and Wootton.

Cromwell was trying to protect the important port of Minehead and perhaps also the parsons he thought to be loyal to his cause (Dr Byam at Luccombe and John Morley at Wootton and Timberscombe.)

In 1642 Dunster became a parliamentary stronghold and the Royalists sent soldiers to demand surrender. Later, the castle changed hands again and was the only place to hold for the king in the West.

West Somerset was mainly on the side of King Charles and therefore Cromwell felt obliged to maintain a strong military force here to keep a firm hold on the county. He billeted soldiers in these five parishes in the Hundreds of Carhampton. It was estimated that there would be about 50 troopers, mostly horsemen, needing hay and oats for their horses, as well as provision for themselves.

John Reed, who for many years sang in the church choir, remembered that "It was a great event when a barrel organ was installed in the church to provide the music for singing.". He could just remember:- "Previously, a bass viol and a clarionet which led the singing and the choir were stationed in a gallery which has long since disappeared. The barrel organ, which has also gone the way of such things a long time ago, had three barrels and played about thirty tunes."

In 1864 the first bishop of Colombo retired and returned to England where, in the Spring of that year, he became rector of Wootton Courtenay, "a secluded village in one of the loveliest vales of Somerset, and there among simple grateful peasantry I made my last English Home" (From "Memorials of Bishop Chapman").

The restoration of the Church which he undertook was a source of great interest during 1865 and 1866. He was responsible for the rebuilding of the chancel and the raising and altering of the tower to accommodate the six bells which still hang there. The old castellated shape more typical of the West Country was replaced by the current belfry which reputedly reminded the Bishop of his cathedral in Colombo.

On October 6th, 1866 the West Somerset Free Press reported:-

"Wootton Courtenay Church was reopened after being restored and beautified at the sole expense of Bishop Chapman, with the exception of a stained glass window given by Miss Hole of Alcombe".

Great changes took place in most of the parishes of the neighbourhood, owing in great measure to the example and influence of the bishop, seconded by that of his admirable curate, Rev. C. Sainsbury, whose whole life and powers of no uncommon order were devoted to the welfare of the parish and neighbourhood. An impetus was thus given to the schools, to missionary interests and to the temperance work, in all of which Wootton Courtenay took the lead at that time. The Dunster Cottage Hospital scheme was first started by Bishop Chapman, aided by Squire Luttrell and other influential neighbours.

On the Bishop's death in 1879 the Porlock Vale magazine contained an article beginning *"Wootton Courtenay has lost the best and kindest of rectors.........."*

In 1885 the March edition of the Minehead and Porlock Vale magazine tells us that the new Rector, Rev. Stanley has come into residence and will *"read himself in on Sunday March 1st."*

On 9th October it was reported that *"The rector of Wootton Courtenay brought home his bride to the rectory where they were received with a most kind and hearty welcome.* The village had been given a festive appearance with arches and decorations of evergreen and flowers and an arch bearing on one side the words "Welcome to the bride and bridegroom", on the other "Health and happiness". Over the rectory gate was the suitable motto "Home, sweet Home."*

In 1900 a vestry and organ chamber were built and a new organ installed at a cost of £500.

There are fragments of a stone cross in the churchyard and a lamp standard which was put in to light the steps and path during the celebrations to mark Queen Victoria's diamond jubilee in 1897.

There is also a fine yew tree. In 1988 the Conservation Society encouraged the listing of ancient yews, and the one in Wootton Courtenay was probably the first in the district to be recorded.

A certificate in the church issued by the Foundation claims that the tree was at that time 640 years old.

Sponsored by the magazine Country Living and supported by the Archbishop of Canterbury and Robert Hardy the actor (who is an authority on the long bow), David Bellamy had for some time been investigating the age of churchyard yew trees. He devised a way of measuring the trunk to give a fairly accurate age of the tree and invited anyone who was interested to measure the yew in their churchyard by finding the circumference of the trunk at two given heights from the base.

Katherine Brown and I found the circumference to be 16 and 18 feet respectively. This is not a record, as the largest tree so far recorded measures 32 feet and is over 1000 years old. According to our measurements, the Wootton Courtenay tree was planted in about 1349, but this is disputed by other researchers.

Another yew tree was planted behind the church to commemorate Queen Elizabeth II's Golden Jubilee year.

Even before the first church was built, there were many yew trees on the site, where pagan festivals had previously been held.

Apparently, before the time of Pope Gregory II in the early 8th century, the dead were usually buried either near the highway, as Roman law directed, or else in places far from the towns, set aside for the purpose. Gradually, as priests and monks began to offer prayers for the dead and to receive gifts for the monastery or church, Cuthbert, Archbishop of Canterbury in 1750 brought the custom of burial grounds, known as churchyards, to England.

Most churchyards had a yew tree. It has always been considered an emblem of mourning and in former times was reckoned to be a valuable tree. The old English yeomen used the wood of yews to make their bows.

The ancient yew tree and the remains of the stone cross in Wootton Courtenay churchyard.

In 1989 the following appeal was made to the parishioners by Mr J.K. "Jan" Ridler:-

"Although the church building has always been well maintained, the Diocesan Architect has advised that the slate roofs need replacing. Damage was sustained in last winter's gales.

The parishioners are already making a most creditable effort, but it is beyond their resources to raise the £50,000 needed. Help from well-wishers is urgently needed and will be gratefully received."

By the year 2000 restoration had been completed.

The Rev. G. Fisher, who became Archbishop of Canterbury, used to stay with the Reeds at the new Brookside Farm. Mrs Fisher's sister was married in All Saints Church

Wootton weddings

Norman and Annie Ball (1915).

Wedding party outside Riverside

Off on honeymoon to Weston-super-Mare

Mr and Mrs 'Jack' Reed (1916)

The cottage subsequently burned down

Hetty and Ron Churchill (1921).

Bill Burnell's 'Tin Lizzie' took them to Higher Brockwell

Mr and Mrs D Stevens (1917)

Betty Down (1950s?)

For many years it was the custom of the village boys to hold back the newlyweds with a rope until the groom threw them enough cash!

Church outings

The Sunday School

The Mother's Union

Chapter Twelve

The Village School

Wootton Courtenay village school. It is now a dwelling house

The earliest records of education in Wootton Courtenay are of Dame's schools in the early 1800s. In 1818 we read of parochial returns relating to the education of the poor, made to the House of Commons, in which the Rev. Scott states: "There are four small day schools in this parish in which about 40 boys and girls are taught, books being supplied from the Society for Promoting Christian Knowledge. A few are taught at the minister's expense. The poorer classes are desirous of more sufficient means for the education of their children."

In 1859 a public elementary school was built at the expense of R.H.Dutton esq., the owner of the manor of Wootton, and in 1869 it was enlarged to accommodate 80 children. However, the Rev. A.H. Fownes Lutterell, vicar of Minehead was not in favour of over education or of keeping boys at school until they were

eleven when they became "educated above their station" and another vicar thought that, if you had a good school, a boy would have learned all that was necessary by the age of eleven "If kept at school later, he will not settle to manual labour, and gets into idle habits."

There was also a growing opinion that damage was being done to boys' education by the taking of time off to help on the land at busy times when "they forgot as much as they remembered". In 1885 the Rev. Charles Sainsbury was concerned about education in his parish of Wootton, saying that not only the boys stayed away from school to work, but also the girls were kept home to look after the rest of the family while their mothers were at work. He noted "Twelve boys with insufficient education, some being unable to read or write, and also seven girls."

To help this situation, night schools were set up. At Wootton Courtenay, apparently, the night school was open for about 22 weeks during the winter, when the basics of reading, writing and arithmetic were taught. In 1902 there is a record of the evening school having received a government grant of two pounds eighteen shillings. In 1904 the night school was closed, but started again in 1910.

In January 1885, the Minehead and Porlock Vale magazine reported *"Wootton School has suffered much from Scarletina, a mild form of scarlet fever. It has been a continual source of worry to all concerned, for no sooner has the school opened after an abatement of the disease than some other home has been visited and in some cases for a second time. The last was the prostration of Miss Pitt, the schoolmistress. We are thankful to say no deaths have occurred, but the loss to the school and funds will be serious"*

In July, 1885, the magazine reported *"HM Inspector paid his annual visit to the Wootton Courtenay School on the 14th April and his report which has now been received is, we are glad to say, highly satisfactory, especially when it is remembered under what disadvantages the school has laboured during the past school year.*

The inspector says "This is an excellent country school, well disciplined and thoroughly well taught in both the elementary and extra subject. With a somewhat more careful style of writing, nothing would remain to be desired from elder school. The infants are, on the whole, well taught, but their knowledge of number is limited."

Since the end of April, Miss Pitt has carried on the work of Wootton School single handed, but it is much to be hoped that a suitable pupil teacher may soon be found to assist in the work, or else it must be feared that in spite of all the Mistresses efforts the school may not earn so good a report next year."

Children of the village school in 1893

In her letter, Bessie Dyke described her school days in the village school in the early 1900s: - *"I was born in 1893 at Ranscombe, eighth child of John and Sarah Hale. I look back on my childhood as the happiest years of my life, went to the little school at the age of three, could read at five and at that time no child left the school who could not read or write. We greatly enjoyed a school outing to Blue Anchor in farm wagons with boards nailed across to sit on. Also Timberscombe club day, saving our few pennies to buy wonderful sugar almonds and gingerbread.*

The school had two rooms, separate entrances for boys and girls, also separate playgrounds. The infants room had wooden benches arranged in a tier; the youngest sat on the lowest bench and as one progressed moved up a bench. The rest of the room was used three days a week for the older girls to learn sewing and knitting.

Both rooms were heated by coke burning large iron stoves. The large room was used not only for school lessons but also for all social occasions. When numbers reached 50, we had our first schoolmaster, a Mr Oates who was also organist at the church. Annie Quick was the schoolteacher. When Mr Oates died, Mr Boddycott was the next schoolmaster. Religious Knowledge was one of the chief subjects taught and every year the Dunster Deanery Diocesan Society set an examination for different ages and my one claim to fame I won first prize for my class every year starting at the age of seven.

The Boer War was being fought in 1901 and we were very patriotic. A large map hung in the large school room and Mr Oates would point with pride at all the countries coloured red, saying it was the British Empire, but also telling us that as
other empires had fallen so also in time would the British Empire. I did not think then that it would be in my lifetime."

Many years later, Harry Roberts, a noted spinner of yarns of Wootton Courtenay recalled another side of school life in late Victorian times when the boys managed to get hold of the schoolmaster's keys, lock the donkey in the school and took the keys down to Lower town where they threw them in the river. What a pity no one had the foresight to record more of Harry's anecdotes.

Mrs Dyke remembered that the schoolroom was not only used for social occasions. On December 4th, 1894, the first parish meeting of Wootton Courtenay was held there. There were fourteen parochial electors present and the Rev. Stanley was elected chairman.

During the First World War the West Somerset Free Press reported on September 23rd 1916 that "The children of Wootton Courtenay School kept a day in honour of Jack Cornwall, the Victoria Cross boy hero of the battle of Jutland. Each child subscribed a penny for the Star and Garter Hospital (for wounded ex-servicemen) at Richmond."

In October of the same year, it was reported that "Somerset Education Committee decided that boys under twelve who had been temporarily exempted from school in order to do farm work should return to school at the end of the month."

At Wootton Courtenay School "Five children had made perfect attendance during the last half year: - Winifred Quick, Beatrice Baker, Albert Carter, Willie Farmer and Thomas Court." Incidentally, with the exception of Winifred Quick, they all remained in the village for the rest of their lives.

Also in September 1916, we learn that the earnings of the schoolchildren at "urt" (whort, or whortleberry) picking during the unusually long season had amounted to thirty pounds, and it is from an article written many years later for the Exmoor Review by Tom Court (he who made the perfect attendance) that the following memories of "urt" picking on Exmoor are taken:-

Before and after the First World War whortleberry or "urt" picking, as it is locally known, was quite an industry. As soon as the whorts were ripe, some of the children would be kept from school to gather them. Children, sometimes accompanied by their mothers, would set off across the moors with a basket and sandwiches (often bread and jam or rhubarb – no butter as the jam alone would soak into the bread and keep it moist) wrapped in a large red handkerchief and, to drink, a bottle of cold tea.

They would walk to Grabbist where the berries grew among the gorse and fingers and legs were very sore at the end of the day, so they were glad when the whorts were ripe on Dunkery, Dunkery Hill Gate and Bincombe. Sometimes they would walk for nearly two hours before picking. The whorts were sold to Mr Tom Webber and his sister who had a horse and cart.*

Whorts were measured into a quart pot and the price was 4d a quart at the beginning of the season, dropping to 3d or 2½d as they became more plentiful. During the war, the price rose to 2s 6d. Money earned was used to buy clothes and boots for the winter, "but," Tom said "we were allowed to keep what money we earned on the last day of urting so we were usually very energetic that day."

Children of the school in 1920

*John Ball remembers that in later years they were sold to Mr Hobbs from Nether Stowey. He had a van in which he carried small barrels for the "urts". When the time came, his arrival was duly announced:-
"old 'obbs 'ave come for the urts."

A letter written by Miss Florence Baker in 1975 describes how she was appointed as head of the two-teacher school in 1920:-

"On a bright April morning in 1920 I arrived Dunster Station for an interview with the Rector with regard to the headship of Wootton Courtenay Church School. A gentleman met me and drove me to the Rectory. On alighting, I was taken into the drawing room, to discover that the gentleman was the Rector himself, which amused him greatly. We soon got down to business. Afterwards I was taken to see the school premises and then back to the Rectory for refreshments. I was pleased to learn I had obtained the appointment. My sister later became the Infants Teacher. We found the children eager to learn and the first pupil to pass the entrance test to a grammar school was Muriel Connibere, who chose Bishops Foxes of Taunton. Her success was followed by Hester Taplin, Robert and Jack Reed and Bessie Quick*, who went to Minehead.

Cookery lessons were introduced for the girls and the instructor was very impressed by their good behaviour and concentration.

The years passed very smoothly until numbers were so low it became a one teacher post and eventually an uncertificated post in the 1930s."

Wootton Courtenay Schoolchildren in 1923

*Bessie (now Bessie Groves) still lives in the district, and has become a poet of some note!

In 1929, an extract from the Parish Meeting Records states:-

"a complaint has been made of the extravagant way the education authorities wasted the ratepayers money in providing new desks and chairs where the old ones were quite good enough"

A question was raised in 1935 as to the discipline of the village schoolchildren. The school managers gave an assurance that they would continue to do everything in their power to see that the children were under proper control.

Douglas Lang recounts that it was questioned whether the only teacher - a nun - could be expected to control the older boys. Some of them, including Douglas, were sent to Dunster , which he said was the best thing that could have happened to him. He never missed a day's schooling there. One day they got soaked on the way to school and felt sure they would have to be sent home, but they were just put in the boiler room to dry out! Discipline was strict: "Parson Lawrence gave the cane"

Jo Collins (née Josephine Quick) is the great niece of Winnie of the perfect attendance and of Bessie the poet. She remembers her wartime years at Wootton Courtenay school:-

"I attended Wootton School from age five to almost eleven. The building was right in the centre of the village, not far from home. Girls and boys had separate entrances to cloakrooms and playgrounds. Once in the classroom we were all together, a complete mix of age groups and abilities which must have been a real challenge for our teacher.

We sat at old-fashioned desks complete with inkwells. Some were double desks

and there was a lot of squabbling to make sure that you avoided sharing with someone you did not like! The inkwells provided good ammunition for firing bits of inky blotting paper off the end of rulers!

It was not very warm in the winter because the only source of heat was a large coke-burning stove, which gave out heat in fits and starts, accompanied by clouds of fumes. The windows were too high for us to see anything except the sky.

My first teacher Miss Warner is a fairly vague memory, but Miss Griffin (later Mrs. Barrow) was a big influence on me. We had a wide-ranging curriculum including English, Maths, History, Geography, Sewing, Knitting, Nature, Gardening, Music, Singing and Religion, all taught by one teacher to all age groups!

I have plenty of memories but at this distance in time it is impossible to put them in chronological order. One special day that stands out is the arrival of the first school radio. It is impossible now to imagine the excitement of listening to our first B.B.C. Schools Programme. (We did not have a radio at home until some time later.) I especially liked the music programmes and a geography series that culminated in the whole school making a model of a Red Indian village, complete with tepees, squaws with papooses on their backs and braves with spectacular head dresses.

Another thing I enjoyed was a series of charts recording the seasons. I can see them now with their brightly coloured pictures of snow scenes, spring flowers, summer sun and autumn leaves. Perhaps living in the countryside, surrounded by the beauties of nature made this all the more relevant.

Then came a wonderful day when we were given a School Garden. This was a fairly large piece of land, half way down Lower Town Hill, opposite the Rectory. The older children were divided into threes and each group given a plot to clear and look after. I revelled in it. I remember being fiercely bossy to the other two over the design of our plot. I insisted that we should include a rockery that turned out to be very difficult to maintain! (They say that you learn by your mistakes but I've still got a small rockery in my garden!)

School dinners were available but I always went home. This was mostly a great bonus but <u>not</u> on wet Mondays. Monday was always washing day. Our kitchen had a copper in one corner, with a fire to heat the water and boil the washing. Next to it was a large mangle to wring out the wet clothes. An awful lot of hard physical work was required even on a fine day. If it was wet the house would be full of steam and wet washing and both Gran and Mum would (understandably) be in a bad mood. To add insult to injury Mondays always meant cold meat and 'bubble and squeak' (potatoes and green vegetables left over from Sunday) for dinner.

The school was a Church school and the Rector was closely involved in school life. Each day began with prayers and a hymn and the Rector came every week to give us scripture lessons. On special days in the Church Calendar e.g. Ash Wednesday, Ascension Day and Saints Days we went across the road into church for services.

Church was very much part of every day life. Most of our family were in the church choir, Mum was secretary of the P. C. C. and a member of the Mothers Union. Many of our relations were buried in the churchyard and we always went with Mum on Saturdays to 'do' the graves - cutting the grass, scrubbing the headstones and putting fresh flowers in the vases. The Church activity that I loved best was decorating for Christmas, Easter and Harvest. At Easter we went out into the lanes to pick masses of primroses to make dozens of small bunches to bury in moss round the font and the pulpit. At Harvest the church was full of the flowers, vegetables and corn from gardens and farms all over the village.

One Christmas memory remains vivid. The school was involved in a Nativity Play to be performed in the church. The play began with the Annunciation. I had the part of the Angel Gabriel, dressed in a white gown, with very precariously fastened silver wings and a halo of wire and tinsel. The pulpit in Wootton church is quite high off the ground. I had been concealed there before the congregation arrived so that I could make a dramatic appearance for the Annunciation scene. Unfortunately the sight of this sudden apparition so startled one of my aunts that she almost fainted and had to be helped to the back of the church to recover!

Another pleasure in church was the Children's Corner. This was a forward thinking innovation on the part of the Rev. Venables. The Corner included an Altarpiece painted by the Art teacher at Minehead Grammar School, the embroidered Mothers Union Banner and a table piled with children's books. I loved the colours on the Altar and the banner and the books were a great attraction to a confirmed bookworm.

There were more serious sides to school and village life because my time at Wootton School coincided almost exactly with the years of the Second World War.

The influx of evacuees into the village caused a few upheavals and made the school extra crowded for a time. These children came from very different backgrounds than ours and were scared at leaving home and ending up living with a lot of strangers. They were much more 'streetwise' than us country children and were deeply suspicious of the whole country set up. Many had never seen a large animal like a cow and they were nearly all afraid of the dark. Remember that we had no electricity in the village at that time and this was compounded by the blackout. After a few skirmishes and fights amongst the boys we all settled down together reasonably well.

Wootton Courtenay schoolchildren in 1941

However many of them soon went back home, although a few stayed and made Somerset their permanent home. The Grammar school in Minehead shared its accommodation with a whole school evacuated from London. This delighted the pupils as they only attended school for half a day but it must have been a nightmare of logistics for the staff.

We had some very unusual lessons including Aircraft Recognition, the history of Army Badges and organised walks to collect rosehips to make rosehip syrup. (This was used as a substitute supply of Vitamin C because oranges were no longer available.)

Most interesting to me was a series of First Aid lessons given by Dr. Anderson, a retired Doctor living in the village. Even at this age I knew I wanted to be a nurse when I grew up, so I thoroughly enjoyed learning to bandage knees, put on a sling and above all to evert an eyelid! While all the others were shuddering at the thought I was busy showing off and imagining myself as a latter day Florence Nightingale.

We had to take our gas masks to school every day and to have drills to make sure we knew how to use them. We had little understanding of the seriousness of all this but we were very competitive about who had the smartest or most highly coloured gas mask case! My sister was furious because she had a slightly smaller head size and this meant that she had to have a 'Mickey Mouse' mask which she considered very babyish.

I suppose the most obvious affect of the war on village life was the small number of men who were still at home. Many were in the forces, with only a minimum kept at home in essential jobs like farming and market gardening. This meant that the women had to help,

particularly at haymaking and harvest. We children did not see this as a problem or a worry, but a joy! We just loved being out in the fields, having picnics, helping (or hindering?) and above all following Blossom and Smart, the vast carthorses, as they pulled loads of hay or corn down to the farmyard to be stacked. As soon as the carts were empty we jumped up in the back and rode back up to the fields. This was a source of great enjoyment and lots of squealing as we went over bumps or better still had to splash across the stream that ran along one side of the farmyard. It was a magic time for us and in hindsight it always seemed to be lovely sunny weather!

Our area was never bombed although we sometimes heard planes on their way to Bristol. A German plane crashed at Timberscombe and some German parachutists landed in the village when they baled out of their damaged plane. We all walked over New Road once to watch a stricken tanker blazing in Porlock Bay.

German and Italian prisoners were brought from the prisoner of war camp at Watchet to help on the farms. Some of them made toys in their spare time. I remember one with a set of beautiful peacocks with painted tails. The birds nodded their heads and appeared to peck when they were rotated. (I cannot remember whether that was a present or if they were for sale.)

We often saw troop convoys come through the village. I remember one in particular with a lot of Bren gun carriers which stayed overnight in the blacksmiths shop. My mother and all the other women in Lower Town made tea for them and we children found it all very exciting. The boys, including my brother were all marching about wearing their toy tin hats and saluting.

We also entered into Home Guard exercises with great gusto. The older children were used as 'casualties', which meant being allowed to stay up late and take part in what seemed to us to be an exciting game - people rushing about with stirrup pumps, whistles, tin hats and bandages.

I'm not trying to make light of the difficulties and heartaches of wartime. There were plenty of those even in our comparatively safe area and life was restricted in many ways.

Even us children were not untouched by all this. In our family we worried constantly about Dad who was at Dunkirk and El Alamein and who we had not seen for several years. When a letter arrived from him that was a real red-letter day and we longed for him to be back home safe and sound.

Most families had loved ones in the forces or in towns that were being destroyed in the bombing.

There was a constant struggle to keep things going without enough people to do the work. Rationing and shortages of just about everything caused continual problems. I think it is a real tribute to the grown ups in the village that my memories can be so full of good things as well as the troubles of wartime and that our childhood was in the main happy and secure."

After the war the number of children in the village school declined until only ten of school age remained. It was obvious that the school could no longer remain open and, to everyone's regret, it was decided that Wootton children would have to attend Timberscombe School. An agreement was made with the county that the children would receive free transport, which was at first provided by cars, and later by bus.

Undoubtedly, the closing of the school was another blow to village life as the old folk knew it.

The school post-war.

Back : Miss Griffin; Bill Lang; David Quick; Andrew Slade; Pam Carter; Archie Dyer

Front: Phyll Quick; Chrissie Brooks; Belinda Jury; Albert Slader

A more informal picture of the same children taken in the school playground on the same day as the photograph on the previous page. Phyllis Quick remembers that the trolley belonged to Bill Lang who always had trolleys around and went on to be a car mechanic. He used to make steam engines and aeroplanes in his garden shed and once blew himself and the shed up!

Back row (l to r):-   Bill Lang, David Quick, Pamela Carter, Andrew Slade

Front row (L to R):- Chrissie Brooks, Phyll Quick, Belinda Jury, Archie Dyer
*   Albert Slader*

Chapter Thirteen

Social Life

Special events

James Savage in the History of the 100s of Carhampton in 1830 recorded that in Wootton Courtenay a fair for cattle and sheep was held here on 19th September. In 1940, John Reed, then 90 years old and an inhabitant of the village all his life, still working as a rate collector for Williton District Council (the same year in which he informed the council he thought it was time for a rise in salary!) described Revel Sunday - the first Sunday after 21st September - and the festivities as follows:-

"There were standings all along the street in Higher Town, gingerbread stalls, sweet stalls, shooting places and so on. Crowds of people used to come there from all parts and they were rough old times. There was no policeman then to keep order. Where Rosemount now stands there was a public house called the Rose and Crown and there was a terrible lot of drinking with the Revels. They used to dance all night, nearly, in a room over the public house. Revels Day brought many wrestlers from all around and even from Devonshire to compete for prizes of money - though not very big prizes. The wrestling took place at one time just below the road where Mr Docker's drive entered" (now the drive to Orchard and Morton Houses). "I can see it now. Before they got hold of one another they would run and kick at each other most dreadful. I've seen two men kick each other so hard as they could, but they had to kick below the knees. Of course, there used to be a referee to see they did it properly.

We used to get some wrestlers from Cutcombe and Timberscombe. I remember one little chap from Cutcombe called Stevens – a splendid little chap, he was – very active and beggared if he wouldn't throw 'em all, and they couldn't put him on his back. There was a chap called Yandle from Timberscombe, Tom Pope of Huntscott and Tom Priscott of Wootton, both splendid chaps." (There are still families bearing these names living in the locality today).

John went on to name men who excelled from surrounding villages - names still born by local families today. However, the coming of Bishop Chapman brought an end to the revels and the rough play and drunkenness that attended them. An article in the West Somerset Free Press of September 1866 reported that: "Drunkenness and debauchery used to attend the ancient festival of harvest at Wootton Courtenay, but all that was now past, thanks to the institution of a dignified Harvest Home celebration by Bishop Chapman, helped by Curate Sainsbury. This year's celebration, however, was a little marred in the morning by some wandering vendors putting up their "standings", but Bishop Chapman firmly held to his rule that there must be no buying or selling and the vendors had to quit."

Under Bishop Chapman, the village improved its moral tone, with the termination of The Revels and the introduction of the Harvest Home celebrations, which included a dinner for the parish and sports, which were usually held in the Parsonage Field. John Reed also remembered that "It was in Bishop Chapman's time that Wootton had a fife and drum band. I was the drummer and later they had a brass band, which used to go round to club walks of other villages. Wootton itself never had a village club"

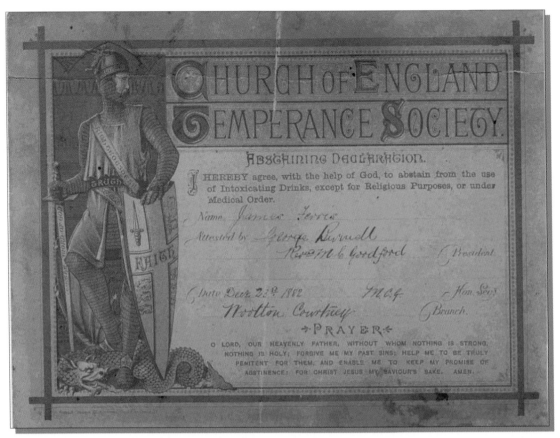

James Ferris's Temperance declaration of 1882

A branch of the Temperance Society was formed in 1876 and two elderly residents recalled that a Temperance Tea was held every November for Adults and children, and the children had an outing in the summer.

The Temperance Tea was always arranged when there was a full moon. The children had tea first and were then sent out to play on the street in the moonlight whilst the adults had their tea. It was voted fine fun by Phoebe Quick and Tom Court, remembering their childhood days.

In July 1890, the Porlock Vale Magazine reported:-

"On June 10th, the adult members of the Wootton Courtenay Temperance Society held their annual excursion; the place chosen was Exeter. A start was made about 6.15 a.m. to drive to Dulverton, where the train was taken for Exeter, which place was reached about 10.30. A considerable part of the morning was spent studying the different parts of the Cathedral, the beauties of which were much appreciated. Many of the party mounted the tower, but the extensive prospect was unfortunately much hidden by mist. The rest of the day was spent in viewing the Museum and other parts of the City. The return home was made by Dulverton again; and, both going and returning, the party was favoured with fine weather for the drive down the beautiful valley. Home was reached about 10.15, after a very enjoyable day. The juvenile members of the Society had an excursion to St Audries on Friday, June 27th."

Temperance outing in the nineteenth century

And in the twentieth (1922)

Nearby Timberscombe had its Friendly Society which reached its centenary in 1923. The anniversaries, or club walks, were a great day for the village and were held at Whitsun, when members and men also from other villages marched round with their colourful floral staves.

Procession leaving Timberscombe

Floral staves

1923 centenary photo

At Ranscombe Farm

In 1897, Queen Victoria's Diamond Jubilee was celebrated. The Parish Council minutes record that £22. 3s. 2d. was subscribed towards proceedings. A thanksgiving service was held on Sunday June 20th and on June 22nd a Bank Holiday dinner and tea were provided in a tent in the Parks (glebe land, now part of the village playing field). The afternoon was spent at sports and games followed by a dance in the School Room. An account of money spent on refreshments is shown below.

Also in the parish records for 1897 is an entry:

"To mark the occasion of Queen Victoria's Diamond Jubilee, a standard lamp was placed in the churchyard to light the steps and path."

The July 1897 copy of the Porlock Vale Magazine records:-

"A very successful celebration of the Queen's Jubilee took place at Wootton Courtenay on June 21. Several helpers had occupied most of the previous day in erecting arches and banners, &c. in various places, giving this quiet village an unusually gay appearance. In the early morning many were awaked by a joyful peal from the church bells and the firing of salutes. The actual celebration of the day began with a procession starting from the school door at 1.30, when, led by the Rector and the Church choir, nearly the whole population proceeded to the Church, singing the National Anthem.

Queen Victoria's Diamond Jubilee Celebrations, 1897

	£	s	d
149 lbs beef	4	19	10
50 loaves &			
75 lbs cake - Mr Burnell	3	1	2½
Sugar "		3	0
Sweets and nuts "		3	10
6 quarts milk		2	6
24 doz lemonade	1	4	0
Tea	6	10	6
10 0z butter		10	6
Quick - fire tending		2	0
A. Court - pony cart		2	0
Mr Chapman, Mr Fairchild		2	0
Band - 4 performances	1	1	0
Prizes for sports	1	15	0
Balance in hand	2	17	11
Given to organ fund			

The accounts for the 1897 jubilee celebrations at Wootton Courtenay

In the church which was so full that some, thinking they could not obtain seats, remained in the porch, the special service of thanksgiving was heartily joined in by all present. After the service a dinner of beef, bread, and a pint of ale, cider, or tea, was partaken of in the school. At the same time a plentiful tea with beef was provided for the children, and others who preferred to join them, in a tent erected in the Park. These refreshments having been disposed of, sports became the order of the day, and were carried on until about 9.15 p.m.; the prizes were then distributed, while an excellent display of fireworks took place under the superintendence of Mr. G. Burnell.

When all was concluded many went up Dunkerry or North Hill to see the bonfires, and thus finish up this most *successful festival. The whole day seemed to pass off pleasantly and enjoyably for all, and many thanks are due to those who in one way or another assisted in the carrying out of the day's proceedings, perhaps not least to those who planned and erected the tent, which afforded a welcome shade from the sun, and where tea and other beverages were supplied throughout the afternoon."*

During the celebrations for the coronation of King George VI in 1937, a meat tea was held in the Village Hall and a commemorative oak tree was planted in the grounds by Mr John Reed and Mr Braunton. Unfortunately, this tree has not survived.

1937 coronation celebrations: catering arrangements (above left); sports in the cricket field (left); Mr Braunton and Mr Reed at the tree planting ceremony (above).

When Queen Elizabeth II was crowned on June 2nd 1953, a service was held in the sports field followed by sports and at 5pm tea was served in the Village Hall for children and adults holding blue tickets. At 6 pm there was tea for all adults holding red tickets and from 6.45 to 7.45 pm a televised view of the Coronation Procession and Abbey Service was relayed to the hall. The television set used was the property of one of the first people in the village to own this new invention. The evening concluded with a concert and social.

A commemorative seat was unveiled at the top of the Church Steps by the Rector, the Rev. Jocelyn Davies and the oldest inhabitant, Mrs E. Williams, who lived in No. 2, Bishop's Cottages.

The Queen's Silver Jubilee was celebrated in 1977 with games and a cricket match in the Cricket Field. Phoebe Quick presented the village children with Jubilee Mugs made by Michael Gaitskell at Mill Pottery and trees were planted at the lower end of the field. This was followed by a party in the Village Hall.

1977 Jubilee celebrations.

1977 Jubilee celebrations: Phoebe Quick presented the Jubilee Mugs. Jack Reed was one of the umpires for the cricket match.. Also in the photo is Gillian Maxfield (receiving a mug), Alison Burnell (next in line), Deborah Dean (behind Alison), Sue Gooding (Between Jack Reed and Deborah Dean), Marjorie Norman (behind Gillian Maxfield) and Joan Norman (on the left of the picture).

A commemorative tree was planted. Phyll Dickens and Jack Reed are chatting in the foreground; Colonel Pitt is third from the left and Carole Turner can just be seen behind him. Maurice Roodhouse is on the extreme right.

On August 2nd 1947, it was recorded that a fete was held which raised £283.11s.2d towards buying a village playing field. The field, which for many years had been glebe land, now belongs to the parish. The entrance is in Butts Lane i.e. The Butts, where archery was practiced; a legal requirement until Stuart times. Actually, in the year 2004 archery is still practiced on the field, which is used by an archery club for practice and matches.

John Reed recalled that the first cricket club was formed when Bishop Chapman was Rector. Apparently, the sport was introduced to Wootton Courtenay by the Rev. Charles Sainsbury, the 'little curate' beloved of all the village after his arrival in 1861. In 1890 a notice in the Porlock Vale magazine gives the result of a match between Wootton Courtenay and Selworthy when Wootton won by 14 runs.

Robert Reed, great grandson of John Reed's brother George, continues the story:

It was in the 1930's and years immediately following the second world war that the club reached its peak. Mr Northropp who was "secretary" to Lady Albrecht at Wootton lodge, became the driving force behind the club. The playing surface was improved and a new pavillion built thanks to the financial assistance of her ladyship. Mr Northropp drove a Rolls Royce!

Wootton Courtenay even entertained Somerset County Cricket Club, featuring the ledgendary Harold Gimblet. This was often on a bank holiday with lunch being taken in the village hall. Wootton Courtenay in the early 1950's possessed some talented players and became one of the foremost Village sides in the area.

Wootton Courtenay versus Timberscombe in 1901. We can only identify Walter Coneybear (arrowed) from the Wootton team. He was a carpenter, who lived at Rose Cottage until his death in the 1950's

125

Wootton Courtenay Cricket Club in the 1930's/40's

Above: at Wootton
    Back: Bill Middleton (umpire); ? ; Peter Hinton; Reg Rawle?; Ralph Hinton; Sam Baker;
                                                        John Ball (Scorer)
    Middle: Reg Court; Mr Northropp; Claude Gooding; Bob Reed.
    Front: Buster May-Brown; George Ball

Below: at Watchet
    Back: Reg Court; Peter Hinton?;R. Rawle?; Alec May-Brown, Ralph Hinton; Charlie Baker
    Seated: Bob Reed; Claude Gooding; Mr Northropp; George Gooding; Buster May-Brown

Photograph taken in 1947 outside the pavilion when Wootton played against a Somerset XI for Frank Lee's benefit.

Frank Lee was a Somerset player who retired from playing in August 1947 and went on to become a first class umpire until 1962

The annual games against local rivals Timberscombe generated much emotion and these were days long before the advent of league cricket! Maurice Huxtable, long time Timberscombe stalwart recalls a remarkable match at Timberscombe. in the early 1950's.

Wootton Courtenay batted first and only scored a paltry 23 all out, although it should be remembered that long grass in the out field made scoring much more difficult than on today's shaved surfaces. At tea Timberscombe had reached 12 for no wicket.

After tea Buster Brown and Charlie Baker, Wootton's main bowlers, switched ends and Timberscombe's batting collapsed being all out for 22 with George Ball taking 3 vital catches. A memorable victory, but it is only fair to note that in later years Timberscombe gained supremacy.

Gradually in the late 1950's and 1960's Wootton found it increasingly difficult to raise a side. Despite this the scorebook shows a famous name appearing for the village in the early 60's.

As a friend of Bruce Heywood who lived nearby, one John Snow, later to become a great Sussex and England fast bowler, was on holiday and was persuaded to play. However, his bowling figures did not foretell his future success on the international stage.

There was a successful youth side in the 1960's but as time went on many of the boys were to leave the area owing to limited employment opportunities, an ongoing trend. The decline continued and the club folded in 1970.

It was the 1977 silver jubilee which led to a revival of the club. A light hearted mens v womens cricket match was held on the playing field and this generated sufficient interest to reform the club. Friendly matches were played in 1978 and then Wootton joined the newly formed West Somerset cricket League. In both 1982 and 1983 Wootton won the Minehead indoor 6's competition defeating strong Minehead, Watchet and Kilve teams in the process.

Also in the 1980's the club gained promotion to top division of the league and won some silverware in 1989 by winning the league knockout cup defeating Fitzhead in the final held at Brompton Ralph.

As in previous times the 1990's saw another decline as it again became increasingly difficult to raise a side and the club folded. Currently there seems little likelihood of a revival although the playing field is still cut regularly and is available for use.

Wootton Courtenay Cricket Club in the early 1980's

Back:
G. Morgan (umpire); D Lang; A Virgin; M Reed; B Adams; P Keal; M Maxfield; C Perry (president).

Front:
N Virgin; B Lang; R Ball (capt); M Keal; D Maiden

Wootton Courtenay - League Knock-out Cup winner, 1989

Back: M Taylor; N Virgin; B Lang; P. Walmsley; M Keal; P Keal.

Front: P Hayes; M Maxfield; R Reed (Captain); J Somers; K Graddon.

Football was also played in Wootton Courtenay for many years. It is not clear when the club was initially founded but there was a village side in the inter war years. With the number of able bodied young men in the village being considerably greater than in more recent times, there was little difficulty in raising a team to compete in the West Somerset League.

During the 1930's, however, the increasing importance of the cricket team brought about a conflict. The football team played across the cricket square and, although the football season was not as long as modern times, nevertheless considerable damage could be done to the cricket playing surface. Apparently the cricket club came out on top as the number of football matches declined.

After the second world war the football club continued for a few years but fielding a competitive team became more and more difficult and the club disbanded in the early 1950's.

In 1967 the enthusiasm of a newcomer to the village, Mr Bill Riley, led to the club being re-formed. No doubt stimulated by England's 1966 world cup success, and the existence of a "glut" of young men from the post war baby boom, a team was entered into the Taunton District Saturday League and some enjoyable seasons ensued. Charlie Parsons later became manager but once more the number of potential players in the village declined and the club disbanded in 1973.

As with cricket, the current age structure of the village population makes it very unlikely that a football team will be forthcoming the future.

Wootton Courtenay football club in the early 30's. Dunkery Hotel in the background
Back row: Bill Middleton; George Channing; ? ;Reg Court; Mr Northropp; ?; ?.
Middle Row: ? ; Stuart Bodley; ?.
Front row: Claude Gooding; ? ; ? ; Raymond Boycott; ?.

The newly reformed Wootton Courtenay Football Club in the late 1960's

Standing: *P Keal (supporter); Bill Riley (Manager); R. Reed; D. Burge; A. Thorne; G. Merson; D Chilcott; R. Routley*

Seated: *J. Jenkins; G. Parsons; R. Sharp; M. Reed; J. Somers; D. Bailey*

During the 1960s Mrs Houlder, who lived at "Crossways" (and was widow of the Houlder Line shipping magnate responsible for the provision of not a little Argentinian corned beef to the UK) paid for a tennis court to be constructed. The main beneficiaries were members of the Ford family. John Ford was rector at the time. His daughter Anna still reads the news! Sadly, there were never enough interested villagers to make full use of the court and it was neglected and eventually removed. In 2004 the field is a popular haunt for dog owners, and a pleasant venue for fetes.

Places of Refreshment

At one time there were two public houses in the village: Bridge Cottage (previously Rawles Cottage) in Lower Town was the Rising Sun. The Rose and Crown, mentioned by John Reed and now known as Stag Cottage, was in Higher Town. It was recorded in the 1861 census with Thomas Knight as Innkeeper. In 1881 a notice of sale read as follows:- "For Sale.

The fully licensed Rose and Crown Inn and six cottages adjoining." Bessie Dyke remembered that " the pub next door was kept by a Mrs Gold," In 1921 the building was known as Rosemount and was bought at the estate sale by Robert Knight, son of Thomas, and Robert and his wife continued to live there. She provided teas for passing travellers.In summer time she would sit at her window, from where she could watch the footpath leading down from Dunkery Beacon to see if walkers were on their way. Then she could be sure to have the kettle boiling when they arrived in the village for a pot of tea and, no doubt, scones with clotted cream and jam.

It is good to know that, in 2002, Janet and Ron Chisholm of The Villagers' Stores opened the Jubilee Café and Tea Gardens where passers-by and local residents can still enjoy a pot of tea and excellent home made scones with clotted cream and jam.*

*The Villagers' Stores has now been taken over by Pam and Russell Hawkins

As we have read, the Dunkery Hotel was built in the late 1890s and George Burnell, a strict Temperance man, provided access to the first floor of his house, Fernlea, so that the men of the village could drink coffee and play dominoes there, rather than go to the bar at the Dunkery. There was speaking tube for them to order the coffee, and the hatch where the dumb waiter used to deliver it still exists.

The Dunkery Hotel, which is now (in 2007) thriving under the ownership of Derek and Beccy Brown

The Village Hall

In the 19th century, the Reading Room (the wooden hut between Wreford and Fernlea which subsequently became the kitchen of the Village Hall), was used mainly by young people for social events, but "never on a Sunday!" Temperance meetings were also held there.

The reading room continued to be used until well into the twentieth century. Douglas Lang , as the youngest boy of the group, was sent up on the roof during a men's club meeting. He carried a wet bag to drape over the smoking chimney.

Subsequent events can be left to the imagination!

Douglas also confirmed another story that Reg Court used to tell when he worked at Brookside: Miss Stretton from Hunscott had left her donkey and cart outside the shop. When she came out again the donkey was still in the shafts, but facing the other way - towards the cart! There had been boys in the vicinity, but as Douglas said, "That's where we disappeared quickly!"

The first proper Village Hall was built in 1931 on land bought from Mr John Reed, as we read previously. The premises were vested in the Trustees of Charity Lands and managed by a council of members appointed by village organisations.

The first 'proper' village hall

In 1950 it was felt that the hall needed upgrading and the following appeal was launched:-

"Dear Sir or Madam

We are appealing to you for your support in our effort to raise £1,000 for alterations and extension to our hall, to consist of adequate heating, the addition of a new kitchen to the existing building, improved cloakroom facilities and storage room and the overhaul of the water and drainage system.

Plans are available for your inspection and we hope to get the heating radiators installed in the autumn.

As the result of our efforts, we are hoping that our hall will emerge as a centre of the social life really worthy of our village. We look forward to your support, for which we thank you in anticipation etc. etc.

Yours…………..

We did it then. We can do it again!

The necessary funds were raised and the improved hall was used for many activities until 1998, when much of the building and its equipment failed to comply with *modern* safety regulations.

It was eventually decided that the old hall should be demolished and a new one worthy of the village built to replace it. Inspired by a dedicated and hardworking committee, the villagers raised money through a variety of activities, donations and bequests and thus became eligible to apply for grants.

The village has good cause to be grateful to the committee members for their efforts in procuring these grants and enabling the splendid new hall to be erected. An opening ceremony was performed by the Explorer Sir Ranulph Fiennes.

The first notable event to take place in the new village hall was the celebration of Queen Elizabeth II's Golden Jubilee, when villagers gathered to enjoy a splendid barbecue.

John Ball, then the oldest lifelong resident of the Village, digs the first sod for the new village hall in 2001. Looking on are: (back row, l to r) Eddie Bishop, Marjorie Giles, Sid Pinder (Chairman); (standing, front row l to r) Janet McEwan, Dorothy Ball, Jenny Maxwell (née Carter), Heather Walker; Sylvia Thwaits; (seated) Anni McEwan

The fine new stage is much appreciated by the village drama society. For many years, plays and concerts have been staged by talented amateur performers in the village The present drama club has the facilities to produce somewhat more polished shows, enjoyed by large audiences as much as ever.

Other organisations have used the hall over the years including, notably, the Women's' Institute (W.I.), whose first meeting was held in November 1932 when Mrs Lucy Reed was appointed as secretary. Miss Maud Vernon, who lived at Allen's Mead, was Somerset County Secretary from 1923 to 1940. Her office was in her home. She has been described as the mother of the Somerset Institute.

(Dorothy Ball was president for many years. She was selected to represent the Institute at the Buckingham Palace Garden party to celebrate the Queen's Silver Jubilee.)

The Women's Institute made a tremendous impact on the village, with the annual flower and produce show being a great event.

Other annual events included the jumble sale to raise funds for the hall and the Church. The queues before opening time were impressive and at least one bargain bought in the 60's is still in use!

When Miss Reed, of Manor Farm, died in 1948, she left money in her will for an annual party for the children of Wootton Courtenay. Also, for some years during the 1960s a special event was the New Year's Eve party and entertainment.

In the early 1960's the hall was used as a venue for the local youth club and Miss Benson who lived at 'West Wind' ran a branch of the County Library. Subsequently, a travelling library served the village.

The hall continues to be the venue for a variety of social activities.

The annual W.I. flower and produce show in the 50's.

Back (l to r) :Rosemary Burnell (Mrs Korda); Mrs H Blackwell; Gwen Jury (Mrs Lovekin); Pam Carter (Mrs Neil).

Front: Mrs Olive Gibbs; Miss 'Emmy' Childs

Drama

The original Wootton Courtenay Dramatic Society was very active during the 1950's and was associated with the Minehead Evening Institute.

In the late 50's and very early 60's several Wootton folk (Tom Court; David and Phyll Quick; Reg and Jemmy Carter) performed in the Luccombe Pantomime. We played at Wootton, Minehead (in the old W.I. Hall at the rear of the General Post Office) and Porlock.

A Dramatic Society Production in the 1950's

Gwen Lovekin (nee Jury), Terry Sizer, Leslie Lewis

Wootton Courtenay Dramatic Society in the 1950's

Back row (L - R)   *Andrew Slade, Gwen Jury, Reg Carter, Leslie Lewis, Belinda Jury, Ella Court, Kathleen Ball, Mrs Kingsnorth, Terry Sizer, Mrs Court , Mrs Annie Ball*

Front row (L - R)   *David Brooks, Dudley Parsons, Vera Payler, Chrissie Brooks, Queenie Brooks, Mr Kingsnorth*

Drama

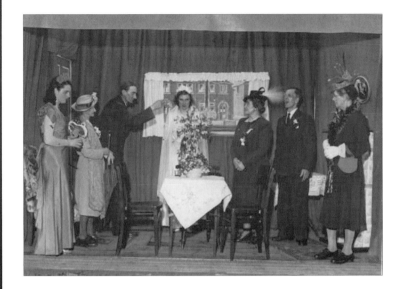

A scene from "Orange Blossom" in the 50's

Gwen Jury,
Annie Ball,
Reg Carter,
Kathleen Ball
Mrs Kingsnorth,
Mr Kingsnorth,
Mrs Court

The Luccombe Pantomime, circa 1960

Below: the cast, including Tom Court (4th from left at rear), Phyll Quick (Principal Boy), Jenny Maxfield—née Carter (Principal Girl) and Walter Play-fair (Dame)

Drama

The Dunkery Players were formed in November 1972 after I had put up a notice inviting anyone interested in forming a drama group to attend a meeting. Our first production in May 1973 was "Quiet Wedding" with a cast of fourteen (something we have never achieved since)!

We have presented one or two full length plays and/or an evening of entertainment most years since.

For most of this time we were, of course, in the old village hall - often half frozen during the winter rehearsals - but still managing to build some stunning sets. Since 2001 we have had the more comfortable facilities in the new hall.

Our current membership is very low, but we are hoping to perform "Living Together" by Alan Ayckbourne in November (2007).

Jenny Maxfield

The Dunkery Players in May 1977

Above:
Standing (L-R): Mike Reed, Cathy Pike, Molly Campion Smith, Mick Maxfield, Phyll Quick, Carole Turner (nee Gooding), Frank Frisby, 'Campy' Campion Smith.

Seated (L-R): Sue Gooding, Peggy Liversage, Frank Liversage, Ray Assinder, Ron Jones, Norma Jones, Ella Frisby

Seated at front: Jenny Maxfield (Nee Carter)

Drama

Wootton Courtenay Pantomime Group

Youngsters from Wootton Courtenay and neighbouring villages put on a series of pantomimes in the early 1990's. They played to packed audiences in the Village Hall and in the process raised hundreds of pounds for the CLIC (the Sargent childhood cancer charity).

Their success was due to the efforts of Daphne Midwood (then at the Dunkery Hotel) and Rita King. Each year the pantomime ran for three nights and a matinee. Pantomimes included Babes in the Wood, Little Red Riding Hood, Snow White and the Seven Dwarfs and Jack and the beanstalk.

Robert Reed

The cast of Snow White and the Seven Dwarfs

Chapter 14

Wootton's 'Grand Old Man'

John Reed was born into a long established Wootton Courtenay family in 1850. He started work as a cobbler at 4 Bishops Cottages, but was a farmer for most of his life at what is now Riverside Farm and subsequently at Brookside Farm. He was a school manager for 36 years, and collected rates for 62 years.

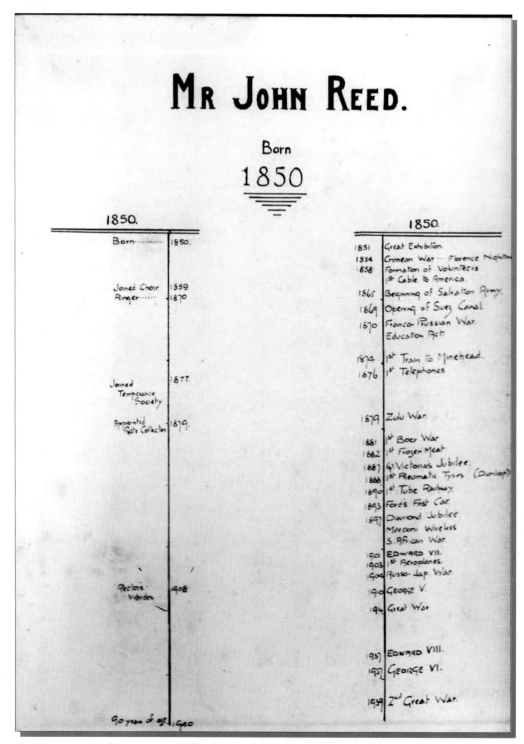

Frontispiece to the album celebrating John Reed's 90 active years.

He lived at Riverside Farm from the age of 8 and farmed there until he had Brookside Farm built in 1921 and he continued in business there (with his son-in-law, Norman Ball) until his death. He sang in the choir for 81 years and was a ringer for 70 years (until about the age of 87), being captain of the tower for many of those years. He was Rector's Warden for 32 years. He continued as a member of the Temperance Society until it disbanded about 60 years after he joined.

Above: John and his wife Martha (née Hale) and daughter Annie at Riverside. Both Annie and her son John Ball in their turn followed John Reed's example as the village's oldest resident.

Left: John in the choir with his grandsons, John and George Ball.

Below: He must have found some time to relax: a picnic with his wife and grandsons.

John Reed was by all accounts a very well loved and respected character, but he could be quite formidable as well! In the early 1930s, Douglas Lang remembers being turfed out of the Cricket Field by John, already in his 80's. They had no business there on a Sunday!

His daughter Annie was engaged to Norman Ball for 13 years and still had a hard time plucking up the courage to tell her father that they had decided to wed. She decided to tell him on the way to Minehead one day, but failed. On the way back she determined she would break the news when they reached the two holly trees (cut down not so very long ago) by Nanny Goat Corner, between Wootton Knowle and Tivington Knowle. John apparently whipped up the horses and they drove home in ominous silence!

John Reed at the age of 90

John Reed's roll-top desk is still used by his great– grandson

One day, when John's grandchildren, John and George Ball , were young, John drank George's medicine to spare him the unpleasantness. John was thrashed and locked in his grandfather's office as a punishment, but he (John Ball) felt so aggrieved that he wreaked further havoc. His grandfather subsequently had to explain to Williton Rural District Council the reason for papers pertaining to the rates having been torn up!

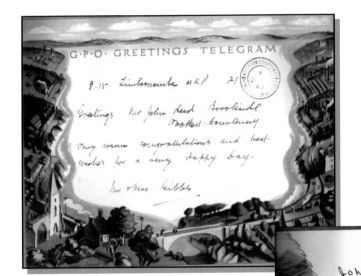

G·P·O· GREETINGS TELEGRAM

9.15 Dunkeswell MK/ 21/

Greetings Mr John Reed Brookside
Wootton-Courtenay

Very warm congratulations and best.
wishes for a very happy day —

Mr & Mrs Gibbs

*Two of the many telegrams
and greeting cards received
by John on his 90th Birthday*

Minehead

John Reed   Wootton Courtenay

Congratulations   and   good   wishes

Allen Thorne

G.P.O.
Greetings Telegram.

*Below: Part of the parish letter
written by the Rector, the Rev. A.P.
Lance, after the 90th birthday
presentation*

Wootton Courtenay   April 1940
Thank you all for the most generous
Easter Offering amounting to exactly
nine guineas that you have given me
I can assure you I appreciate it very much
indeed —
Last week we were all offering Mr John
Reed our congratulations and good
wishes — It was fitting that the
members of the Choir - Ringers - Church
Council and School managers should
join together in doing this; and a
very happy little meeting we had at
the Rectory on March 28th —
It is one thing to reach the age of 90
but another to be willing to continue to
sing in the choir and to hold such important offices as Churchwarden and School
manager to say nothing of carrying on
as we all know Mr Reed does, with other
work not connected with the Church —
It is a very difficult thing to grow old
well - Mr Reed is setting a splendid
example of how to do this, to those of us
who are nearing or who have passed
our 'three score years and ten —
Friday April 5th at 3pm Monthly wartime
Intercession Service
Sunday Ap. 7th will be the M.U corporal Com

John's 90th birthday also marked his 81 years in the choir, 32 years as rectors warden and 36 years as a school manager. At a ceremony in the Rectory Miss Eames presented John with a silver mounted walking stick. She had herself been 60 years in the choir. Mr George Reed had served 50 years, Mrs Stanbury 48 years, Mr W Copp 41 years and Mr W Conybeare, 29 years all without a break. Mrs Conybeare had served 41 years and Miss Sally Kingdon 22 years, each with one break. This made a total of 350 years service!

A letter from Canada

Toronto
May 12/40

Mr John Reed
 Dear Sir

You will no doubt be surprised to receive a few lines from far away Canada, especially from an old resident of your village and my birthplace and I thought this may be a good opportunity to renew old acquaintance after a lengthy time of fifty six years since I left your village and my home.

It happened this way. I was listening one evening to the Toronto daily news cast over my radio when I heard the name of John Reed of Wootton Courtenay mentioned. This made me sit up and take notice, they were giving your record as rate collector for the past sixty two years so I turned to the Daily star and found published just what they had broadcasted and I thought it may be interesting to you to see your record published in a newspaper in far away Canada so I decided I would send it to you, I hope you have not forgotten the Clatworthy family who has been so long extinct from your village. I have not heard from anyone in the village since my Father and Mother died and that is many years ago, both my brothers George and Jim were back home since I left and I myself have not yet given up hope of again visiting my old home town once more. I must congratulate you on your ninety years of age and hope you may carry on for many more yet. I myself am close to eighty one years old and enjoy the best of health. I hear there has been some new buildings put up since I left a new hotel and

a building in the centre of the town where Mr Burgess Carpenter shop used to be. I don't forget the many enjoyable nights we used to put in ringing the Old year out and the New Year in with yourself at the first bell and myself at the third with your brothers Edward and Henry and Will standing. I hear that your brother Edward upon retiring returned to Wootton Courtenay and built himself a house. This is some years ago. I heard of it when my bro Tom returned from a trip over home. Please remember me to Edward and Henry and anyone such as Henry and Alfred Prescott Blacksmiths and the Roberts family and any other old resident who might still be there. I myself am still going strong able to look after my property and attend to my garden. I do not regret leaving home although it was a hard struggle for a number of years but finally I managed to pull out of the rut. I have enclosed the piece which appeared in the paper about yourself in the (Toronto Daily Star) Please remember me to all your family and others who may remember me. Yours truly

Alfred Clatworthy
472 Delaware Avenue
Toronto Canada

John achieved national and international fame just after his 90th Birthday by asking for a rise, which he was granted. He continued with his many duties and many thought he would reach his century.

However, his birthday celebrations had proved a little too much for him and a few months later he died—in harness as he would have wished. He had been delivering rate receipts the day before.

Press reports of John's request for a pay rise at the age of 90

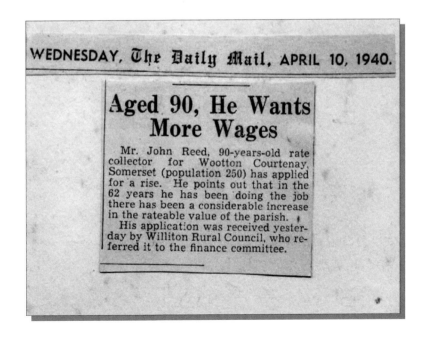

Wootton's Water

Until the end of the 19th Century, villagers obtained their water from wells. The heads of at least three of these survive, including one half way up lower town steep (above) and one at Highpark (below)

Wootton's Water

The remains of the standpipe in Lower Town

When the first public water supply was provided, villagers still had to walk to obtain their water from standpipes, such as the one on the wall of Pound Cottage and another by the roadside at the end of Butts Lane in Lower Town.

By the time the estate was sold in 1920 most properties had their own supply at least to the outside of the house.
Originally, water was piped from a spring in a bog on the moor above Ford Farm. As shown in the parish meeting records, a reservoir was built over the spring in the early 1930's, but the associated works caused the spring to move, and the reservoir never functioned.

For about 30 years, a 200 gallon galvanised tank served quite adequately as a reservoir supplying pure, fresh water for the whole village.

By the mid 60's, some of the higher properties, including the Dunkery Hotel, were complaining of inadequate water supply. The bore of the supply pipe was found to be severely constricted by corrosion, and it was decided to replace it.

In September 1965 a notice announced the closure of the road through Lower Town for "three weeks, or in case of unforeseen circumstances a maximum of six weeks." The road remained closed for six months, during which time at least two crews and their foremen came and went. The first foreman had a man on his books who only had one lung and could not work ("I thought the West Country air would do him good.") and several men who did not exist! The next foreman spent his money and time on drink and harassing the local ladies.

Wootton's Water

The structure over the spring which moved when the reservoir was built

By 2007, the reservoir was completely overgrown, and little except the perimeter wall could be seen

At one stage all the holes in the road containing the connections to individual houses had been filled in, but he had them dug up again because he had lost his glasses. ("The lenses would probably be broken, but I thought I could save the frames.").

The connection to Brookside Farmhouse was tarred over, and was thus inaccessible when it was needed when a tap washer broke in the kitchen. Peter Ball was told "There can't be a connection there because it's not on our plans", so he had to dig it up himself.

Eventually, the entire pipeline to the village was replaced except for the first 300 yards leading from the supply! Not surprisingly, none of this helped the Dunkery Hotel or its neighbours, and it was decided that a new reservoir would have to be built. An 80,000 gallon tank was constructed some way down the valley from the original reservoir. Unfortunately, since water was now being stored, it was necessary to chlorinate it, and they fitted a chlorine drip, which functioned continuously even when water was not being drawn! The first flush of the morning at Brookside made the house reek of chlorine, and the water from the churn cooler bleached the dairy floor!

Not long afterwards, Wootton lost its independent supply and was connected to the national Grid.

Wootton's Weather

The severe winter weather of 1940 was recorded in the parish records.

In 1947, there were again heavy snowfalls and severe frosts lasting for several weeks.

On Boxing Day 1962 snow started to fall on already frozen ground. There was a series of blizzards and the ground remained snow covered until March. Many of the roads were impassable at times and for several weeks children attending school in Minehead had to be billeted there during the week.

The winter of 1947 : Burnell's Taxis (above) and the frozen waterfall at Riverside (below)

Highertown in January 1963

Wootton's Weather

In 1963 Riverside waterfall froze again (above). Stile Road (left) and Ranscombe Road (below) were among those blocked by drifts.

Wootton's Weather

The snow could be fun, and it could be attractive, as scenes from Brookside in 1963 demonstrate.

Wootton's Weather

On October 15th, 1960, many parts of Somerset were flooded. During the day 4.06 inches of rainfall were recorded. At Ford Farm, a rick weighing 5 or 6 tons was moved several yards by the torrent and cattle had to be roped and rescued from the outbuildings.

The torrent flooded Brookside farm yard. The milking machine motor and pump were swamped and, for several days, the cows had to be driven to Burrow to be milked. They were not happy and nor was Martin Ball's teacher, who thought that he was being worked too hard before school in the morning!

Brookside Farm yard (right) and the remains of the wall opposite Crockfords (below)

Water completely surrounded Rawles (now Bridge) Cottage and came in through the back window as well as in and out of the doors. A layer of sand and silt about two feet deep had to be dug out of the ground floor on the following day.

The flood demolished about 30 feet of wall opposite Crockfords and then divided, about half of it continuing along the road past the forge and down Duck Street to meet the main stream at Riverside.

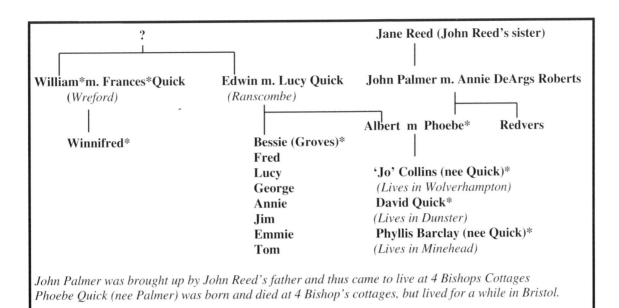

?   **Jane Reed (John Reed's sister)**

William* m. Frances* Quick   **Edwin m. Lucy Quick**   **John Palmer m. Annie DeArgs Roberts**
(Wreford)   *(Ranscombe)*

Winnifred*   **Albert m Phoebe***   **Redvers**

Bessie (Groves)*
Fred
Lucy   **'Jo' Collins (nee Quick)***
George   *(Lives in Wolverhampton)*
Annie   **David Quick***
Jim   *(Lives in Dunster)*
Emmie   **Phyllis Barclay (nee Quick)***
Tom   *(Lives in Minehead)*

*John Palmer was brought up by John Reed's father and thus came to live at 4 Bishops Cottages
Phoebe Quick (nee Palmer) was born and died at 4 Bishop's cottages, but lived for a while in Bristol.*

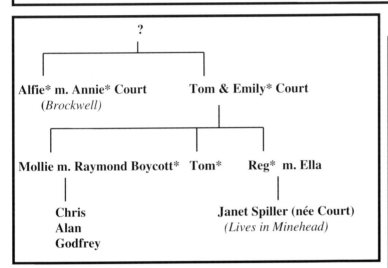

?

Alfie* m. Annie* Court   **Tom & Emily* Court**
(Brockwell)

Mollie m. Raymond Boycott*   **Tom***   **Reg* m. Ella**

Chris   **Janet Spiller (née Court)**
Alan   *(Lives in Minehead)*
Godfrey

Sam & Edie Baker

'Beat' m Dudley Parsons*
Dorothy
Hetty m 'Sonny' Carter*
May Floyd (née Baker)
Nancy
Edith m Cuthbert Perry*
Kath Lang (Née Baker)
Charlie*
Ron*
Joyce Decima m Douglas Lang*

Sam and Edie lived at Rawles Cottages, owned by the Normans at Burrow Farm, for whom Sam worked. His son Ron subsequently worked for the Normans and lived in the cottage with his wife Audrey and sons, Keith and Phillip. It is interesting that in 1842 the house - then 'The Rising Son' - was listed under the name of Thomas Baker.

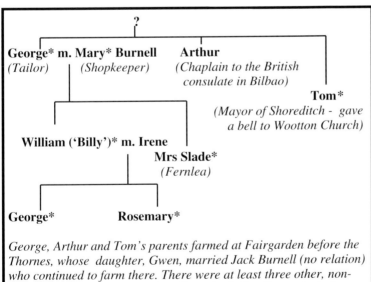

?

George* m. Mary* Burnell   **Arthur**
(Tailor)   *(Shopkeeper)*   *(Chaplain to the British consulate in Bilbao)*

                 Tom*
          (Mayor of Shoreditch - gave a bell to Wootton Church)

William ('Billy')* m. Irene
      Mrs Slade*
      (Fernlea)

George*   **Rosemary***

George, Arthur and Tom's parents farmed at Fairgarden before the Thornes, whose daughter, Gwen, married Jack Burnell (no relation) who continued to farm there. There were at least three other, non-related, Burnell families in the village, including Dave, the baker.

Connections

* Characters mentioned in, or contributing to, the book

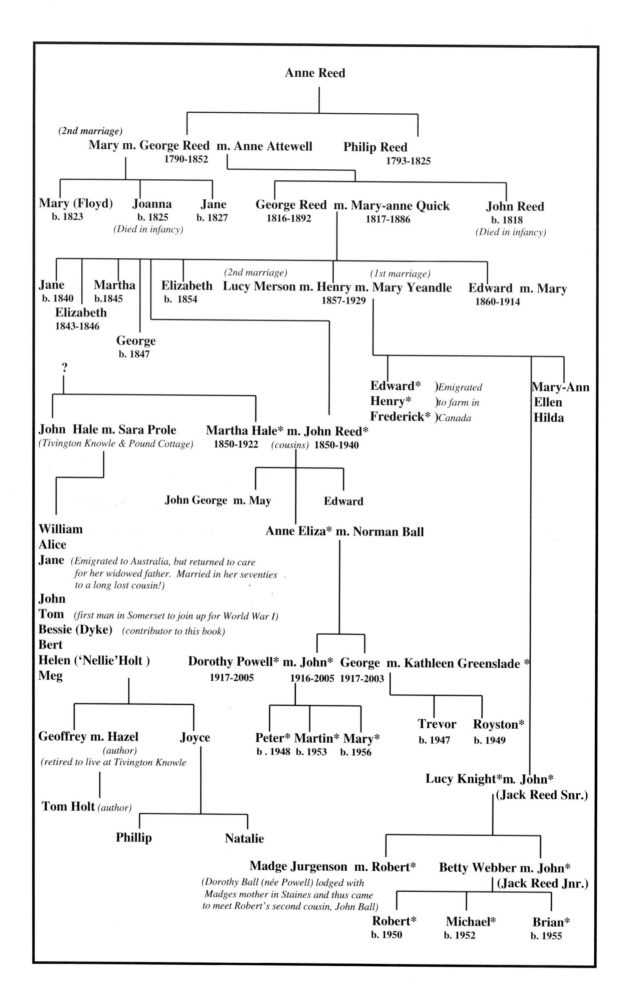

Anne Reed

(2nd marriage)

Mary m. George Reed m. Anne Attewell
1790-1852

Philip Reed
1793-1825

Mary (Floyd)
b. 1823

Joanna
b. 1825
(Died in infancy)

Jane
b. 1827

George Reed m. Mary-anne Quick
1816-1892   1817-1886

John Reed
b. 1818
(Died in infancy)

Jane
b. 1840

Martha
b.1845

Elizabeth
b. 1854

(2nd marriage)
Lucy Merson m. Henry m. Mary Yeandle
1857-1929

(1st marriage)

Edward m. Mary
1860-1914

Elizabeth
1843-1846

George
b. 1847

?

Edward*   )*Emigrated*
Henry*   )*to farm in*
Frederick*)*Canada*

**Mary-Ann
Ellen
Hilda**

John Hale m. Sara Prole
(Tivington Knowle & Pound Cottage)

Martha Hale* m. John Reed*
1850-1922   *(cousins)* 1850-1940

John George m. May

Edward

**William
Alice
Jane** *(Emigrated to Australia, but returned to care*
for her widowed father. Married in her seventies
to a long lost cousin!)
**John
Tom** *(first man in Somerset to join up for World War I)*
Bessie (Dyke) *(contributor to this book)*
**Bert
Helen ('Nellie'Holt)**
Meg

Anne Eliza* m. Norman Ball

Dorothy Powell* m. John* George m. Kathleen Greenslade *
1917-2005   1916-2005 1917-2003

Trevor
b. 1947

Royston*
b. 1949

Geoffrey m. Hazel   Joyce
(author)
(retired to live at Tivington Knowle

Peter* Martin* Mary*
b . 1948 b. 1953   b. 1956

Tom Holt *(author)*

Lucy Knight*m. John*
⌐*(Jack Reed Snr.)*

Phillip   **Natalie**

Madge Jurgenson m. Robert*
(Dorothy Ball (née Powell) lodged with
Madges mother in Staines and thus came
to meet Robert's second cousin, John Ball)

Betty Webber m. John*
⌐*(Jack Reed Jnr.)*

Robert*
b. 1950

Michael*
b. 1952

Brian*
b. 1955